Visions of the Past

▼ ▼ ▼

Visions of the Past

*The Challenge of Film to Our
Idea of History*

▼ ▼ ▼

ROBERT A. ROSENSTONE

HARVARD UNIVERSITY PRESS
Cambridge, Massachusetts
London, England
1995

Library of Congress Cataloging-in-Publication Data

Rosenstone, Robert A.
  Visions of the past : the challenge of film to our idea of his-
tory / Robert A. Rosenstone.
     p. cm.
  Includes bibliographical references and index.
  ISBN 0-674-94097-0 (alk. paper)
  ISBN 0-674-94098-9 (pbk.)
  1. Motion pictures and history. 2. Historical films—History
and criticism. I. Title.
PN1995.2.R67 1995
791.43'658—dc20   95-6720

for Nahid
messenger

Contents

▼ ▼ ▼

III. The Future of the Past

Visions of the Past

▼ ▼ ▼

Introduction

Personal, Professional, and (a Little) Theoretical

The essays in this volume chart the encounter of a professional historian with motion pictures—specifically with films that are consciously historical in their subject matter, films that attempt to represent the past. Any such encounter is bound to be shaped by the particular background, training, experience, and taste—in both history and film—of a single person. Yet no academic is an island, detached from the concerns of a larger social, political, cultural, and intellectual world. In putting these essays together into a single volume, I am betting that my own interest in the historical film resonates throughout the community of historians; that my own concerns parallel some broader concerns of the historical profession; that— dare I be so bold?—these essays represent the meeting of traditional historical consciousness with the increasingly insistent demands of the visual media.

Thirty years ago, when I completed my doctorate, the idea that historical film might be worthy of attention as a medium for seriously representing the past was unthinkable. One might love movies, one might even love historical movies (I didn't), but certainly none of us in graduate school and none of the scholars with whom we studied would have been able to imagine a day when it would be possible, as a historian, to take such works seriously. This personal recollection is underscored by *That Noble Dream* (1988), Peter Novick's lengthy survey of American historical practices in the last century. In close to six hundred pages, the book has but a single reference to motion pictures, and that, typically, is a letter of complaint—from the historian Louis Gottschalk in 1935 to the president of MGM about the low quality of historical films and the need for scholarly consultants in order to make them more accurate.[1]

Times have changed—drastically. Now major journals like the *American Historical Review* and the *Journal of American History* devote sections to film, and the *AHR* has published multi-article forums on such works as *JFK* and *Malcolm X*. Now the American Historical Association and the Organization of American Historians both give awards for the best historical film of the year. Now panels on film and screenings mark every major convention of historians—the AHA, OAH, the Latin American, Middle Eastern, and American Studies Associations. Now institutions such as New York University, the Rutgers Center for Historical Analysis, UCLA, the California Historical Society, the New England Foundation for the Humanities, and the University of Barcelona sponsor major conferences on history and film.

All this activity has hardly made history and film into a field. At best it is a kind of tendency. Or a series of tendencies, for historians deal with film in at least three distinct ways. The two most popular of these— the history of film as art and industry, and the analysis of film as a document (text) that provides a window onto the social and cultural concerns of an era—are well within the boundaries of traditional historical practice. Far more radical in its implications is the investigation of how a visual medium, subject to the conventions of drama and fiction, might be used as a serious vehicle for thinking about our relationship to the past. This approach characterizes the essays in this volume and distinguishes it from other works on history and film.

My own interest in how films work as history began— as has the interest of many historians—in the classroom. In 1970 I started to introduce films into my courses as a way of getting my students, who seemed increasingly reluctant or unable to read history, to "see" the past and "experience" what it was like to live in other times. So well did film work as a teaching technique that in 1977 I created a course in History on Film. The immediate cause was clear enough. From

the mid-sixties into the seventies, my most popular
course had been on the History of Radicalism. In the
middle of the decade enrollments began to dwindle
until there came a term when a single student took
the class. My first offering in History on Film, subtitled
"Radicalism and Revolution," was based on a two-part
strategy: first, get students to confront historical issues
by using the screen to evoke a sense of involvement
in the past and, second, critique the errors and shortcomings of the film by comparing it to written treatments of the same subject. It worked. Enrollments
shot up. Films like *The Organizer, Oktober, Joe Hill,* and
The Battle for Algiers helped to create student interest
in the writings both of theorists (Marx, Lenin, Gramsci, Fanon) and of academics who analyzed the histories of radical movements.

What had an effect on the students ultimately had a
greater effect on their professor. The process of comparing film to the written word in the classroom (History on Film moved on to other topics—Modern
America, Japan, the Soviet Union) led inevitably to
larger questions about the relationship between the
moving image and the written word, about exactly
what could be learned from watching history on the
screen. When two of my own books were used as the
basis of motion pictures, certain questions became
more pressing. What exactly happens to history when
words are translated into images? What happens
when images transcend the information that can be
conveyed in words? Why do we always judge film by

how it measures up to written history? If it is true that the word can do many things that images cannot, what about the reverse—don't images carry ideas and information that cannot be handled by the word?

The problematics raised by film ran parallel to those raised by my main writing project of the eighties. During most of that decade I was creating a narrative that included a search for a new way of expressing the relationship between the historian and his material, between the present and the past. The story I was constructing told how the beliefs, values, and perceptions of three Americans had been altered by living and working in nineteenth-century Japan. In telling the tale, I wanted to find new ways of getting close to my subjects, of seeing through their eyes and expressing the immediacy of moments in their lives. At the same time, I wished to share with my readers the problems of the historian: problems of weighing evidence, making sense out of random data, explaining the inexplicable, and constructing a meaningful past. By incorporating (too timidly I now think) some of the techniques of modernist and postmodernist writers, I eventually produced a multivoiced work set in both the past and the present that simultaneously told a history and problematized its own assertions.[2]

These experiments with narrative grew out of a feeling that traditional forms of history were too limited and limiting. If my innovations were largely intuitive, it is true that even intuitions are structured by one's environment. Toward the conclusion of the project I began to learn what so many people in the human sciences (but too few historians) already knew—that philosophers, literary and cultural critics, narratologists, and postcolonial theorists had for years been pointing to the epistemological and literary limitations of traditional history. Their theories, which seemed to justify my efforts toward a new kind of written history, also suggested that film might be another legitimate way to represent the past.

To begin writing about film meant to change from being a creator of history to being a commentator on histories created by others. This ran counter to my original aim in becoming a historian: to tell stories from the past. The tension between these two impulses may account for many of the differences between my essays and those of other historians who write on film. My desire has been less to critique than to chart the possibilities of the historical film: to understand from the inside how a filmmaker might go about rendering the past on film. Being in such a place is dangerous for the scholar. It results in a kind of complicity, an identification that leads directly to a notion at once obvious and heretical: that the very nature of the visual media forces us to reconceptualize and or broaden what we mean by the word, history.

For all the conferences, articles, and reviews, few historians have been much concerned with exploring the visual media as a way of rendering the past. None has done so systematically, and none has envisioned a role for the specifically historical film. This is true of the two major scholars who deal with the topic, Marc Ferro and Pierre Sorlin. Ferro's best-known work, *Cinema et Histoire,* a series of occasional essays, treats contemporary filmmakers like Jean-Luc Godard as historians who provide a counter-analysis to the studies of society undertaken by academics.[3] Sorlin's more comprehensive volume, *The Film in History,* devotes more space to explaining why historical films reflect their own periods than to how they represent the past.[4] Other scholars have tended to write in a similar vein. No academics seem willing to consider the possibility that filmmakers may have as much right to think about the past as do historians.

The academic or Dragnet historian ("Just the facts, ma'am") looking at film has to face difficult questions: What criteria are applicable for judging visual history? How does film contribute to our sense of the past? The easiest answer (and most irrelevant because it ignores the change in the medium) is to assess how true a work remains to "the facts." But you do not have to see many films to know such an approach is ridiculous in the extreme. Films that have been truest to the facts (never mind which facts or how they have been constituted) have tended to be visually and dramatically inert, better as aids to sleep than to the acquisition of historical consciousness. The all-time snoozer of this genre was PBS' *Adams Chronicles.* In a strange effort at historical veracity, this series utilized as dialogue only words that had actually been written by the appropriate member of the Adams family—without acknowledging the obvious fiction involved in collapsing the difference between the spoken and written word.

Writing on the historical film gave me license to boldly go where no historian had gone before. To seek out new forms of historical film all over the world. To learn that the tradition of film based on events and people of the past is almost as an old as the medium. "Historicals" were among the first films to be made in many countries—India, Japan, France, Russia, China—but are such works history? Most "historicals" have followed the example of Hollywood, where history has usually meant costume drama, a tale of romance and passion set in an exotic past. But everywhere, including Hollywood, there have always been pockets of resistance, filmmakers who avoided the conventions of the popular film, directors like Carl Dreyer, Sergei Eisenstein, and Roberto Rossellini. Their best works—*Joan of Arc, Oktober, The Rise of Louis XIV, The Age of the Medici*—have treated the past as a site less of adventure than of social meaning.

The tendency toward making serious historical films that such directors represent has grown in recent decades as filmmakers around the world have begun to ask questions of the past that are more like the questions traditional historians have wanted to answer: how did we (this state, this region, this people, this gender) get where we are, and what does it mean to be here? These questions are posed within the limits of the medium and its practices—they are asked and answered in images as well as words, in dramatic structures, in personal conflicts, by witnesses and talking heads, answered at twenty-four frames a second in a relentless medium that will not pause for a question until its tale is told.

In many places (Africa, Germany, Latin America, Eastern Europe, Russia), filmmakers have been making a conscious attempt to resurrect pasts that the mainstream cinema has always ignored or reconfigured. By giving voice to the voiceless, some of these have created a filmic equivalent of the New Social History. This tendency, so evident in the low-budget documentary of many lands, has also marked the dramatic feature. Today it is easy to name a host of directors whose major works center on historical questions: Carlos Diegues (Brazil), Rainer Werner Fassbinder (Germany), Tomás Gutiérrez Alea (Cuba), Hsou Hu (Taiwan), Alexander Kluge (Germany), Akira Kurosawa (Japan), Glauber Rocha (Brazil), Jorge Sanjinés (Bolivia), Ousmane Sembene (Senegal), Masahiro Shinoda (Japan), Oliver Stone (United States), Istvan Szabo (Hungary), Paolo and Vittoria Taviani (Italy), Marguerite von Trotta (Germany), Andrzej Wajda (Poland), Zhang Zhimou (China).

To think systematically about historical film is to find that at least one other discipline has already staked out the ground: cinema studies. For the historian, it is not an easy task to engage this discourse, one complete with its own vocabulary, agenda, goals, and boundaries. Unlike most history, cinema studies is highly theoretical at its core. It is true that, in recent years, the field has been seeking a new object of study, or attempting to find a new ground in something its practitioners like to call history. But the historian should not be fooled by this familiar word. Theorists in cinema studies (as well as those in such fields as literature, narratology, feminism, postcolonialism) do not mean quite the same thing as do historians when they use the word "history." Rarely, for example, do they refer to events, facts, data—to the traces of the past with which the historian attempts to reconstruct a vanished world. The focus tends to be on the creation and manipulation of the meanings of the past, on a discourse that is free of data other than that of other discourses, on what seems to be the free play of signifiers signifying history.

The history named by theorists can be, at first, baffling to the Dragnet historian. It seems to be history that cares about how the past means without caring about the things which happened in the past that give rise to the meaning. Yet for the historian interested in film, it is crucial to come to grips with such thinking. The encounter with theory forces us to wonder about the telling more than the told, about the elements that comprise history, about how they cohere into images of and meanings from the past.

From reading too much theory, the Dragnet historian may begin to feel a touch of vertigo. But there is no doubt that a dose of theory is good for us. At the very least, it helps bring to consciousness many things that we historians should already know, but things that, as we become absorbed in our stories, we like to forget. That all history, including written history, is a construction, not a reflection. That history (as we practice it) is an ideological and cultural product of the Western World at a particular time in its development. That history is a series of conventions for thinking about the past. That the claims of history to universality are no more than the grandiose claims of any knowledge system. That language itself is only a convention for doing history—one that privileges certain elements: fact, analysis, linearity. The clear implication: history need not be done on the page. It can be a mode of thinking that utilizes elements other than the written word: sound, vision, feeling, montage.

Viewing too many historical films raised another problem for me, similar to the one I had with written history. The form of the standard historical film began to seem too much like the standard written history, which, in its conventions of realism, incorporates the aesthetic values of the nineteenth-century novel. Dramatic films and documentaries deliver the past in a highly developed, polished form that serves to suppress rather than raise questions. Too often such works do little more than illustrate the familiar. Rarely do they push beyond the boundaries of what we already know. Certainly the best standard historical films may do something for history by showing, personalizing, and emotionalizing the past, and delivering it to a new audience. But this is not, I feel, to use the capabilities of the medium to their fullest. In no way do such films do what film might do: offer a new relationship to the world of the past.

The limitations of the standard film became obvious as I encountered a far more interesting kind of historical work, one which uses the medium to revision, even reinvent History. This is what I call the postmodern history film, a work that, refusing the pretense that the screen can be an unmediated window onto the past, foregrounds itself as a construction. Standing somewhere between dramatic history and documentary, traditional history and personal essay, the postmodern film utilizes the unique capabilities of the media to create multiple meanings. Such works do not, like the dramatic feature or the documentary, attempt to recreate the past realistically. Instead they point to it and play with it, raising questions about the very evidence on which our knowledge of the past depends, creatively interacting with its traces. And yet such films understand that, however much we may problematize our knowledge, the one thing we cannot do is banish the past and do away with the burden of the histories we carry.

The essays in this volume are on occasion like these postmodern history films—fragmentary, partial, playful, or incomplete. In truth, they are not meant to be seen as definitive statements on any topic, but as forays, explorations, provocations, insights. They certainly do not and are not meant to add up to a unified argument, but point toward the issues of historical film—What are they? What is the world they create? How may one judge them?—as well as toward the issue of how one might write about film. Taken together, they are part of a search for a method of getting at these moving artifacts that always seem to escape our words, that overflow with more meaning than our discourse can contain.

One way of seeing this collection is as an intervention into a field that does not quite yet exist—a strike into an area that may someday revolutionize our notions of the past. Since the essays trace the course of a historian's ongoing interactions with the visual media, the ideas in them rarely stay neatly within the boundaries of a single piece. Notions hinted at in one essay are often continued, illustrated, and more fully worked out in another. One could consider them as constituting a single, exploratory work, divided into ten chapters. To help guide the reader, these are, in turn, subdivided into the following three sections:

History in Images: The two most general pieces about the larger issues of historical film, dramatic or documentary. "History in Images / History in Words" opens the major questions surrounding historical films— what they are, how they work, why we should care about them. "The Historical Film" includes an attempt to show how we can assess and evaluate the contribution of historical film to our sense of the past.

The Historical Film: Detailed readings of five individual films, to show how they work as pieces of History.

Included here are two standard dramas *(Reds, JFK)*, one standard, talking-heads documentary *(The Good Fight)*, and two highly innovative, postmodern history films, one which pushes the boundaries of dramatic history toward new visual vocabularies *(Walker)* and the other which creates history as a multilayered vision *(Sans Soleil)*.

The Future of the Past: Three explorations of the new kind of history film that forces us to reconceptualize what we mean when we say "history." "Revisioning History" deals with the innovative strategies of films made in Africa, Latin America, and Germany. "The Future of the Past" delineates the contours of the postmodern history film as practiced by some innovative and thoughtful filmmakers. "What You Think About When You Think About Writing a Book on History and Film" ranges the world musing on the possibilities of the history film in many cultures.

Taken together, the essays point toward two major claims which I wish to highlight here. Claims whose implications, if taken seriously, are not easy for historians to accept:

A film is not a book. An image is not a word. This is easy to see (and say) but difficult to understand. At the very least it means that film cannot possibly do what a book does, even if it wanted to do so. And, conversely, a book cannot do what film does. Those films that try most literally to render the past lose the power of the medium. The larger point: the rules to evaluate historical film cannot come solely from written history. They must come from the medium itself—from its common practices, and how they intersect with notions of the past. The rules of visual history have yet to be charted. (I try to point towards some of them.)

Film is history as vision. The long tradition of oral history has given us a poetic relationship to the world and our past, while written history, especially in the last two centuries, has created an increasingly linear, scientific world on the page. Film changes the rules of the historical game, insisting on its own sort of truths, truths which arise from a visual and aural realm that is difficult to capture adequately in words. This new historical past on film is potentially much more complex than any written text, for on the screen, several things can occur simultaneously—image, sound, language, even text—elements that support and work against each other to render a realm of meaning as different from written history as written was from oral history. So different that it allows one us to speculate that the visual media may represent a major shift in consciousness about how we think about our past.

A final point: if the study of film has been part of a search for new ways to express a relationship to the past, it is natural that some of the pieces are not standard essays, but play with the essay form—avoiding linear argument to move toward knowledge fragments that make an argument by agglomeration, inference, collage. This introduction itself, with its mixture of the personal, professional, and theoretical, all in disconnected paragraphs, no doubt issues from a mentality influenced by the structure and form of film—particularly postmodern film. Such an aesthetic is part of an attempt to make the reader, like the film viewer, share in the author's process of creating meaning from the encounter with historical films. It also may suggest how an interest in film can help restructure our notion of what it is to tell a story or to write a historical essay.

I
HISTORY IN IMAGES

▾ ▾ ▾

· 1 ·

History in Images
History in Words

Reflections on the Possibility of Really Putting History onto Film

My initial attempt to look at the broad issues posed for the historian by film, this essay was the first piece on historical film to be published in the American Historical Review. *Like many of the essays to follow, it is a mixture of personal and theoretical concerns. So much difficulty did I have in keeping the ideas in line that in its original form, the piece consisted of thirty-four numbered and disconnected paragraphs. The editor insisted the* AHR *could not publish it unless the paragraphs were glued together in normal scholarly form. This did not make them more coherent, but it may well have kept readers from being even more upset than they were at the invasion of the journal by discussions of this new medium.*

A Historian in Filmland

For an academic historian to become involved in the world of motion pictures is at once an exhilarating and disturbing experience. Exhilarating for all the obvious reasons: the sex appeal of the visual media; the opportunity to emerge from the lonely depths of the library to join together with other human beings in a common enterprise; the delicious thought of a potentially large audience for the fruits of one's research, analysis, and writing. Disturbing for equally obvious reasons: no matter how serious or honest the filmmakers, and no matter how deeply committed they are to rendering the subject faithfully, the history that finally appears on the screen can never fully satisfy the historian as historian (though it may satisfy the historian as film-goer). Inevitably, something happens on the way from the page to the screen that changes the meaning of the past as it is understood by those of us who work in words.

The disturbance caused by working on a film lingers long after the exhilaration has vanished. Like all such disturbances, this one can provoke a search for ideas to help restore one's sense of intellectual equilibrium. In my case the search may have been particularly intense because I had a double dose of this experience—two of my major written works have been put onto film, and both times I have been to some extent involved in the process.

The two films were almost as different as films can be. One was a dramatic feature and the other a documentary; one was a $50 million dollar Hollywood project and the other a $250,000 work funded largely with public money; one was pitched at the largest of mass audiences and the other at the more elite audience of public television and art houses. Yet despite these differences, vast and similar changes happened to the history in each production, changes that have led me to a new appreciation of the problems of putting history onto film. After these experiences I no longer find it possible to blame the shortcomings of historical films on either the evils of Hollywood or the woeful effects of low budgets, on the limits of the dramatic genre or on those of the documentary format. Today I feel that the most serious problems the historian has with the past on the screen arise out of the nature and demands of the visual medium itself.

The two films are *Reds* (1982), the story of the last five years in the life of the American poet, journalist, and revolutionary John Reed, and *The Good Fight* (1984), a chronicle of the Abraham Lincoln Brigade, that unit of American volunteers who took part in the Spanish Civil War. Each is a well-made, emotion-filled work that has exposed a vast number of people to an important historical subject previously known largely to specialists or to old leftists. Each brings to the screen a great deal of authentic historical detail. Each humanizes the past, turning long-suspect radicals into admirable human beings. Each proposes—if a bit indirectly—an interpretation of its subject, seeing political commitment as both a personal and historical category. Each connects past to present by suggesting that the health of the body politic and, indeed, the world depends upon such recurrent commitments.

Despite their very real virtues, their evocations of the past through powerful images, colorful characters, and moving words, neither of these motion pictures can fulfill many of the basic demands for truth and verifiability used by all historians. *Reds* indulges in overt fiction—to give just a couple of examples—by putting John Reed in places where he never was, or having him make an impossible train journey from France to Petrograd in 1917. *The Good Fight*—like so many recent documentaries—tends to equate memory with history; it does this by allowing veterans of the Spanish Civil War to speak of events more than four decades in the past without calling their misremembrances, mistakes, or outright fabrications into question. And yet neither fictionalization nor unchecked testimony are the major reasons that these films violate my notions of history. Far more unsettling is the way that each tends to compress the past into a closed world by telling a single, linear story with essentially a single interpretation. Such a narrative strategy obviously denies historical alternatives, does away with complexities of motivation or causation, and banishes all subtlety from the world of history.

This sort of criticism of history on film might be of no importance if we did not live in a world deluged with images, one in which people increasingly receive their ideas about the past from motion pictures and television, from feature films, docudramas, miniseries, and network documentaries. Today the chief source of historical knowledge for the bulk of the population— outside of the much-despised textbook—must surely be the visual media, a set of institutions which lies almost wholly outside the control of those of us who devote our lives to history.[1] Any reasonable extrapolation suggests that trend will continue. Certainly it is not farfetched to foresee a time (are we almost there?) when written history will be a kind of esoteric pursuit; when historians will be viewed much like the priests of a mysterious religion, commentators on sacred texts, and performers of rituals for a populace little interested in their meaning but indulgent enough (let us hope) to pay for them to continue.

To think of the ever-growing power of the visual media is to raise the disturbing thought that perhaps history is dead in the way God is dead. Or at the most alive only to believers—that is, to those of us who pursue it as a profession. Surely I am not the only one to wonder if those we teach or the population at large really know or care about history, the kind of history that we do. Or to wonder if our history—scholarly, scientific, measured—fulfills the need for that larger History, that web of connections to the past that holds a culture together, that tells us not only where we have been but also suggests where we are going. Or to worry if our history really relates us to our own cultural sources, tells us what we need to know about other traditions, and provides enough understanding of what it is to be human.

Perhaps it seems odd to raise such questions at this point in time, after two decades of repeated methodological breakthroughs in history, innovations that have taught us to look at the past in so many new ways and have generated so much new data. The widespread influence of the *Annales* school, the New Social History, quantification and social science history, women's history, psychohistory, anthropological history, even the first inroads of continental theory into a reviving intellectual history—all these developments indicate that history as a discipline is flourishing. But—and it is a big but, a but that can be insisted on despite the much discussed "revival of narrative"—it is clear that at the same time there is a rapidly shrinking general audience for the information we have to deliver and the sorts of stories we have to tell. Despite the success of our new methodologies, I fear that as a profession we know less and less how to tell stories that situate us meaningfully in a value-laden world. Stories that matter to people outside our profession. Stories that really matter to people inside the profession. Stories that matter at all.

Enter film: the great temptation. Film, the contemporary medium still capable of both dealing with the past and holding a large audience. How can we not suspect that this is the medium to use to create narrative histories that will touch large numbers of people? Yet is this dream possible? Can one really put history onto film, history which will satisfy those of us who devote our lives to understanding, analyzing, and recreating the past in words? Or does the use of film necessitate changing what we mean by history, and would we be willing to make such a change? The issue comes down to this: is it possible to tell historical stories on film and yet not lose our professional or intellectual souls?

Can History Really Be Put onto Film?

Thirty years ago Siegfried Kracauer, a theoretician of both film and history, dismissed the historical feature as stagy and theatrical, in part because modern actors looked unconvincing in period costumes, but in larger measure because everyone knows—he argued—that it is not really the past on the screen but only an imitation of it.[2] If he neglected to deal with the equally obvious shortcoming of written history, or to explain why we so easily accept the convention that words on a page are adequate to the task of showing us the past, Kracauer at least made a stab at the theoretical problems of history on film. This is more than you can say of recent scholars. Despite a great deal of professional activity concerning history and the visual media—the articles and monographs, the panels at major conventions, the symposia sponsored by the AHA, New York University, and the California Historical Society—I have encountered but two discussions of what seems a most basic question: can our written discourse can really be turned into a visual one?[3]

R. J. Raack, a historian who has been involved in the production of several documentaries, is a strong advocate of putting history onto film. Indeed, in his view film seems to be perhaps a more appropriate medium for history than the written word. Traditional written history, he argues, is too linear and too narrow in focus to render the fullness of the complex, multidimensional world in which humans live. Only film, with its ability to juxtapose images and sounds, with its "quick cuts to new sequences, dissolves, fades, speed-ups, [and] slow motion" can possibly hope to approximate real life, the daily experience of "ideas, words, images, preoccupations, distractions, sensory deceptions, conscious and unconscious motives and emotions." Only film can provide an adequate "empathetic reconstruction to convey how historical people witnessed, understood, and lived their lives." Only film can "recover all the past's liveliness."[4]

The philosopher Ian Jarvie, the author of two books on motion pictures and society, takes an entirely opposite view. The moving image carries such a "poor information load" and suffers from such "discursive weakness" that there is no way to do meaningful history on film. History, he explains, does not consist primarily of "a descriptive narrative of what actually happened." It consists mostly of "debates between historians about just what exactly did happen, why it happened, and what would be an adequate account of its significance." While it is true that a "historian could *embody* his view in a film, just as he could embody it in a play," the real question is this: "How could he defend it, footnote it, rebut objections and criticize the opposition?"[5]

Clearly history is a different creature for each of these two scholars. Raack sees history as a way of gaining personal knowledge. Through the experience of people's lives in other times and places, one can achieve a kind of "psychological prophylaxis." History lets us feel less peculiar and isolated; by showing that there are others like us, it helps to relieve our "lone-liness and alienation."[6] This is hardly the traditional academic view of the subject, but if one looks at history as a personal, experiential way of knowing, then Raack's arguments seem to make sense. Certainly he is right that, more easily than the written word, the motion picture seems to let us stare through a window directly at past events, to experience people and places as if we were there. The huge images on the screen and wraparound sounds tend to overwhelm us, swamp our senses and destroy attempts to remain aloof, distanced, or critical. In the movie theater we are, for a time, prisoners of history.

That, for Jarvie, is just the problem: a world that moves at an unrelenting twenty-four frames a second provides no time or space for reflection, verification, or debate. You may be able to tell "interesting, enlightening, and plausible" historical stories on the screen, but you cannot provide the all-important critical elements of historical discourse—you cannot evaluate sources, make logical arguments, or systematically weigh evidence. With those elements missing, you have history that is "no more serious than Shakespeare's Tudor-inspired travesties." This means that virtually all filmed history has been "a joke," and a dangerous one at that. A motion picture may provide a "vivid portrayal" of the past, but its inaccuracies and simplifications are practically impossible for the serious scholar "to correct."[7]

If most academic historians are likely to feel closer to Jarvie than to Raack, it is still necessary to ask to what extent his arguments are true. Take the notion that the "information load" of film is impoverished. Surely this depends upon what one means by "information," for in its own way film carries an enormously rich load of data. Some scholars claim not only that an image of a scene contains much more information than the written description of the same scene, but that this information has a much higher degree of detail and specificity.[8] One does not need to be an expert to discover this—all one need do is attempt to render into words everything that might appear in a single shot from a movie like *Reds*. Such an assignment could easily fill several pages, and if this is the case with a single shot, how much more space would be needed to describe what goes on in a sequence of images? The real question thus becomes not whether film can carry enough information, but whether that information can be absorbed from quickly-moving images, is really worth knowing, and can add up to "history."

What about Jarvie's assertion that history is mainly "debates between historians"? Certainly scholars do continually disagree over how to understand and interpret the data of the past, and their debates are important for the progress of the discipline—one might even say that debates help to set the agenda for research by raising new issues, defining fields, refining questions, and forcing historians to check each other's accuracy and logic. And certainly it is true that each and every work of history does take its place in a discourse that consists of pre-existing debates, and the very meaning of any new work is in part created by those debates even if they are not acknowledged within the work itself.

The question for history on film, however, is not whether historians always, or usually, or even sometimes debate issues, or whether works take their place in a context of ongoing debates; the question is whether each individual work of history is, or must be, involved in such debates, and involved so overtly that the debate becomes part of the substance of the historical work? To this question the answer is "No." We all can think of works which represent the past without ever pointing to the field of debates in which they are situated; we all know many excellent narrative histories and biographies that mute (or even moot) debates by ignoring them, or relegating them to appendices, or burying them deep within the storyline. If written texts can do this and still be considered history, then surely an inability to "debate" issues cannot rule out the possibilities of history on film.

The Dramatic Feature

When historians think of history on film, what probably comes to mind is what we might call the Hollywood historical drama like *Reds,* or its European counterpart *The Return of Martin Guerre* (1983)—the big-budget production in which costumes, "authentic" sets and locations and well-known actors tend to take precedence over attempts at historical accuracy. Such works in truth fall into a genre that one might label "historical romance." Like all genres, this one locks both filmmaker and audience into a series of conventions whose demands—for a love interest, physical action, personal confrontation, movement towards a climax and denouement—are almost guaranteed to leave the historian of the period crying foul.

Yet this need not be so. Certainly in principle there is no reason why one cannot make a dramatic feature set in the past about all sorts of historical topics—individual lives, community conflicts, social movements, the rise of a king to power, revolutions, or warfare—that will stay within the bounds of historical accuracy, at least without resorting to invented characters or incidents. If by its very nature, the dramatic film will include human conflict and will shape its material in accordance with some conventions of story-telling, this does not entirely differentiate it from much written history. One may argue that film tends to highlight individuals rather than movements or the impersonal processes that are the subject of a good deal of written history, yet we must not forget that it is possible to make films that avoid the glorification of the individual and present the group as protagonist. This was certainly one of the aims and accomplishments of Soviet filmmakers in the twenties in their search for non-bourgeois modes of representation. If the best known of their works—Sergei Eisenstein's *Battleship Potemkin* (1925) and *Oktober* (1927)—are for political reasons skewed as history, they certainly provide useful models for ways to present collective historical moments.

To represent history in a dramatic feature rather than a written text does involve some important tradeoffs. The amount of traditional "data" that can be presented on the screen in a two-hour film (or even an eight-hour miniseries) will always be so skimpy compared to a written version that covers the same ground that a professional historian may feel intellectually starved. Yet the inevitable thinning of data on the screen does not of itself make for poor history. On many historical topics, one can find short and long and longer works, for the amount of detail used in a historical argument is arbitrary, or is at least dependent upon the aims of one's project. Certainly Jean-Denis Bredin's recent book, *The Affair,* though four times as long, is no more "historical" than Nicholas Halasz's earlier *Captain Dreyfus,* and Leon Edel's one-volume *Henry James* no less "accurate" than his full six-volume version.

If short on traditional data, the screen does easily capture elements of life which we might wish to designate as another kind of "data." Film lets us see landscapes; hear sounds; witness strong emotions as they are expressed with body and face, or physical conflict between individuals and groups. Without denigrating the power of the written word, one can claim for each medium unique powers of representation. It seems, indeed, no exaggeration to insist that for a mass audience (and I suspect for an academic elite as well) film can most directly render the look and feel of all sorts of historical particulars and situations—say farmworkers dwarfed by immense Western prairies and mountains, miners struggling in the darkness of their pits, millworkers moving to the rhythms of their machines, or civilians sitting hopelessly in the bombed-out streets of cities.[9] Film can plunge us into the drama of confrontations in the courtroom or the legislature; the simultaneous, overlapping realities of war and revolution; the intense confusion of men in battle. Yet in doing all this, in privileging visual and emotional data and simultaneously downplaying the analytic, the motion picture is subtly—and in ways we don't yet know how to measure or describe—altering our very sense of the past.

The Documentary

The other major type of history on film comes under the label of documentary. Yet whether it is the film compiled of old footage and narrated by an omniscient voice (the voice of history), a film that centers on talking heads, either survivors remembering events or experts analyzing them, or some combination of the two, the historical documentary—just like the dramatic feature—tends to focus upon heroic individuals and, more important, to make sense of its material in terms of a story that moves from a beginning through a conflict to a dramatic resolution. This latter point cannot be too strongly emphasized. All too often historians who scorn dramatizations are willing to accept the documentary film as a more accurate way of representing the past, as if somehow the images appear on the screen unmediated. Yet the documentary is never a direct reflection of an outside reality, but a work consciously shaped into a narrative which—whether dealing with past or present—creates the meaning of the material being conveyed.

That the "truths" of a documentary are not reflected but created is easy to demonstrate. Take, for example, John Huston's famed *Battle of San Pietro* (1945), shot during the Italian campaign in 1944 with a single cameraman. In this film, as in any war documentary, when we see an image of an artillery piece firing followed by a shell exploding, we are viewing a reality created only by a film editor. This is not to say that the shell fired by the gun that we saw did not explode somewhere, or that the explosion did not look pretty much like the one that we saw on the screen. But since no cameramen could follow the trajectory of a shell from gun to explosion, what we have in fact seen are images of two different events spliced together by an editor to create a single historical moment. And if this happens with such a simple event, how much more does it mark complicated events which are shown to us in actuality footage?

As a form capable of conveying history, the documentary has other limits as well. Some of them are highlighted by my experience with *The Good Fight*. In writing narration for this film, I was frustrated by the directors in my attempt to include the issue of possible Stalinist "terrorism" in the ranks. Their reasons were as follows: (a) they could find no visual images to illustrate the issue and were adamant that the film not become static or talky; and (b) the topic was too complex to handle quickly, and the film—as all films—had so much good footage that it was already in danger of running too long. This decision to sacrifice complexity to action, one that virtually every documentarist would accept, underlines a convention of the genre: the documentary bows to a double tyranny—which is to say, an ideology—of the necessary image and perpetual movement. And woe be to those elements of history which can neither be illustrated nor quickly summarized.

The apparent glory of the documentary is that it can open a direct window onto the past, allowing us to see the cities, factories, landscapes, battlefields, and leaders of an earlier time. But this ability also constitutes its chief danger. However much film utilizes footage (or still photos, or artifacts) from a particular time and place to create a "realistic" sense of the historical moment, we must remember that on the screen we see not the events themselves, and not the events as experienced or even as witnessed by participants, but selected images of those events carefully arranged into sequences to tell a particular story or to make a particular argument.

Toward a Visual History

Historians can easily see how such film conventions of both the dramatic feature and the documentary shape or distort the past in part because we have written work by which the piece of visual history can be judged. What we too easily ignore, however, is the extent to which written history, and especially narrative history, is also shaped by conventions of genre and language. This needs to be underscored. So many scholars have dealt with questions of narrative in recent years that narratology has become a separate field of study. Here I only wish to call to mind a few of their insights that seem relevant to history on film: (a) Neither people nor nations live historical "stories;" narratives, that is, coherent stories with beginnings, middles, and endings, are constructed by historians as part of their attempts to make sense of the past. (b) The narratives that historians write are in fact "verbal fictions;" written history is a representation of the past, not the past itself. (c) The nature of the historical world in a narrative is in part governed by the genre or mode (shared with forms of fiction) in which the historian has decided to cast his story—ironic, tragic, heroic, or romantic. (d) Language is not transparent and cannot mirror the past as it really was; rather than reflecting it, language creates and structures history and imbues it with meaning.[10]

If written history is shaped by the conventions of genre and language, the same will obviously be true of visual history, though in this case the conventions will be those of visual genres and visual language. To the extent that written narratives are in fact "verbal fictions," then visual narratives will be "visual fictions"—that is, not mirrors of the past but representations of it. This is not to argue that history and fiction are the same thing, nor to excuse the kind of outright fabrication that marks Hollywood historical features. History on film must be held accountable to certain standards, but—and this is the important point—these standards must be consonant with the possibilities of the medium. It is impossible to judge history on film solely by the standards of written history, for each medium has its own kind of necessarily fictive elements.

Consider the following: in any dramatic feature, actors assume the roles of historical characters, and provide them with gestures, movements, and voice sounds that create meaning. Sometimes, in fact, film must provide a face for the faceless, such as that South African railway conductor, undescribed in Gandhi's autobiography, who pushed the young Indian out of a train compartment for whites and started him on the road to activism. In such cases, certain "facts" about individuals must be created. Clearly this is a fictive move, yet surely no real violence is done to history by such an addition to the written record, at least not so long as the "meaning" that the "impersonators" create somehow carries forth the larger "meaning" of the historical character whom they represent.

To begin to think about history on film not simply in comparison with written history but in terms of its own is not an easy task. Current theories of cinema—structuralist, semiotic, feminist, or Marxist—all seem too self-contained and hermetic, too uninterested in the flesh-and-blood stuff of the past, the lives and struggles of human individuals and groups, to be directly useful to the historian. Yet the insights of theoreticians do offer valuable lessons about the problems

and potentialities of the medium; they also point towards some of the important differences between the
way words on the page and images on the screen
create versions of "reality," differences that must be
taken into account in any serious attempt to evaluate
history on film.[11] At the very least, historians who
wish to give the visual media a chance will have to
realize that because of the way the camera works and
of the kinds of data that it privileges, history on film
will of necessity include all sorts of elements unknown
to written history.

New Forms of History on Film

Although they are currently the most common forms,
it would be a mistake to take the big Hollywood feature or the standard documentary as the only possible
ways of doing history on film. In recent years, directors from a variety of countries have begun to make
movies that convey some of the intellectual density
that we associate with the written word; films which
propose imaginative new ways of dealing with historical material. Resisting traditional genres, these
filmmakers have moved towards new forms of cinema
which are capable of exploring serious social and political issues. The best of such films present the possibility of more than one interpretation of events—they
render the world as multiple, complex, and indetermi-
nate, rather than as a series of self-enclosed, neat,
linear stories.

The names of these innovative filmmakers are not

well-known in the United States outside of specialized cinema circles, but some of their works are available here. For the historian interested in the possibility of complex ideas being delivered by film, the most interesting and provocative of such works may be the feature-length *Sans Soleil* (1982). Impossible to summarize in words, this best-known work of Chris Marker, an American who lives in Paris, is a complex and personal essay on the meaning of contemporary history. The film juxtaposes images of Guinea-Bissau and the Cape Verde Islands with those of Japan in order to understand what the filmmaker calls "the poles of existence" in the late twentieth-century world. It can also be seen as a kind of oblique investigation of Marker's contention (made in the narrative) that the great question of the twentieth-century has been "the coexistence of different concepts of time."[12]

Far from Poland (1984), made by Jill Godmilow, is another good example of how film can render historical complexity. An American who had spent some time in Poland, Godmilow was unable to get a visa to go there to make a "standard" documentary on Solidarity. Staying in New York, she made a film anyway, a self-reflexive, multilevel work, one that utilizes a variety of visual sources to create a highly unusual "history" of Solidarity—actuality footage smuggled out of Poland, images from American television newscasts, "acted" interviews from original texts that appeared in the Polish press, "real" interviews with Polish exiles in the United States, a domestic drama in which the filmmaker (read "historian") raises the issue of what it means to make a film about events in a distant land, and voice-over dialogues of the filmmaker with fictional Fidel Castro, who speaks for the possibility of contemporary revolution and the problems of the artist within the socialist state. Visually, verbally, historically, and intellectually provocative, *Far from Poland* tells a good deal about Solidarity and even more, perhaps, about how Americans reacted to and used the news from Poland for their own purposes. Not only does the film raise the issue of how to represent history on film, it also provides a variety of perspectives on the events it covers, thus both reflecting and entering the arena of debates surrounding the meaning of Solidarity.

The topics of both Marker and Godmilow may be contemporary, but the presentational modes of their films are applicable to subjects set more deeply in the past. Nor are documentarists the only filmmakers who have been seeking new ways of putting history onto the screen. All historians who feel a need to resist the empathic story told in Hollywood films, with its "romantic" approach and its satisfying sense of emotional closure, will find themselves at one with many Western radical and Third World filmmakers who have had to struggle against Hollywood codes of representation in order to depict their own social and historical realities.[13] In some recent Third World historical films, one can find parallels to Bertold Brecht's "epic" theater, with its distancing devices (such as direct speeches or chapter headings for each section of a work) that are supposed to make the audience think about rather than feel social problems and human relationships.

Though the filmmakers are no doubt working from

a native sense of history and aesthetics, this is what seems to happen in such works as Ousmane Sembene's *Ceddo* (1977) and Carlos Diegues' *Quilombo* (1984), both of which present historical figures with whom it is impossible to identify emotionally. Made in Senegal, *Ceddo* portrays the political and religious struggle for dominance that occurred in various parts of Black Africa during the eighteenth and nineteenth century, when a militant Islam attempted to oust both the original native religion and the political power structure. The Brazilian film *Quilombo* presents a history of Palmares, a remote, long-lived, seventeenth-century community created by runaway slaves that for many decades was able to hold off all attempts of the Portuguese to crush its independence. Each film delivers its history within a framework of interpretation—*Ceddo* upholds the pre-Islamic values of Black Africa, and *Quilombo* glorifies the rich tribal life of a culture freed of the burden of Christian civilization.[14]

For anyone interested in history on film, the chief importance of these works may lie less in their accuracy of detail (I have been unable to find commentaries on them by specialists in their fields) than in the way they choose to represent the past. Because both films are overtly theatrical in costuming and highly stylized in acting, they resist all the usual common-sense notions of "realism" that we expect in movies like *Reds*. Clearly the camera in these films does not serve as a window onto a world that once existed; clearly it represents something about the events of the past without pretending to accurately "show" those events. Yet just as clearly, each of these films is a work of history which tells us a great deal about specific periods and issues of the past.

In their unusual forms, *Ceddo* and *Quilombo* work to subvert a major convention of history on film, its "realism." At the same time, they also highlight, and call into question, a parallel convention of written history: the "realism" of our narratives, a realism based—as Hayden White showed two decades ago—on the model of the nineteenth-century novel. It is possible, in fact, to see these works as examples (in a different medium) of what White was calling for when he said that if history were to continue as an "art," then to remain relevant to the issues of our time historians would have to move beyond the artistic models of the nineteenth century. *Ceddo* and *Quilombo* may be products of Third World nations, but they point the way towards the narrative forms of the twentieth century, towards the necessity for modernism in its many varieties (expressionism, surrealism, etc.), or even postmodernism, as modes of representation for dramatizing the significance of historical data.[15]

The Challenge of the Visual

Almost a century after the birth of the motion picture, film presents historians with a challenge still unseized, a challenge to begin to think of how to utilize the medium to its full capabilities for carrying information, juxtaposing images and words, providing startling and contrastive mixtures of sight and sound, and (perhaps) creating analytic structures that include visual elements. Because its own conventions are so strong and, to the historian, so initially startling, the visual media also serve to highlight the conventions and limitations of written history. Film thus points towards new possibilities for representing the past, possibilities that could allow narrative history to recapture the power it once had when it was more deeply rooted in the literary imagination.[16]

The visual media present the same challenge to history that they have to anthropology, where the ethnographic documentary, born as a mode of illustrating the "scientific" findings of written texts, has in recent years cut loose from its verbal base to seek what one scholar calls "a new paradigm, a new way of seeing, not necessarily incompatible with written anthropology but at least governed by a distinct set of criteria."[17] Now it seems time for such a "shift in perspective," one occasioned by the opportunity to represent the world in images and words rather than in words alone, to touch history. Doing so, it will open us to new notions of the past, make us ask once more the questions about what history can or cannot be. About what history is for. About why we want to know about the past and what we will do with that knowledge. About possible new modes of historical representation, both filmic and written—about history as self-reflexive inquiry, as self-conscious theater, as a mixed form of drama and analysis.

The challenge of film to history, of the visual culture to the written culture, may be like the challenge of written history to the oral tradition, of Herodotus and Thucydides to the tellers of historical tales. Before Herodotus there was myth, which was a perfectly adequate way of dealing with the past of a tribe, city, or people, adequate in terms of providing a meaningful world in which to live and relate to one's past. In a postliterate world, it is possible that visual culture will once again change the nature of our relationship to the past. This does not mean giving up on attempts at truth, but somehow recognizing that there may be more than one sort of historical truth, or that the truths conveyed in the visual media may be different from, but not necessarily in conflict with, truths conveyed in words.

History does not exist until it is created. And we create it in terms of our underlying values. Our kind of rigorous, "scientific" history is in fact a product of history, our special history which includes a particular relationship to the written word, a rationalized economy, notions of individual rights, and the nation state, and many cultures have done quite well without it. Which is only to say that there are, as we all know but rarely acknowledge, many ways to represent and relate to the past. Film, with its unique powers of representation, now struggles for a place within a cultural tradition which has long privileged the written word. Its challenge is great, for it may be that to acknowledge the authenticity of the visual is to accept a new relationship to the word itself. We would do well to recall Plato's assertion that when the mode of the music changes, the walls of the city shake. It seems that to our time is given this vital question to ponder: if the mode of representation changes, what then may begin to shake?

· 2 ·

The Historical Film

Looking at the Past in a Postliterate Age

This essay began as a presentation to a conference on the broad theme of "How We Learn History in America," held at the University of North Carolina. While others wrestled with major issues of the profession—the historical canon, Western civilization courses, textbooks, how to teach race and gender—I used the occasion to explore the question of how film creates a world of the past that must be judged on its own terms. Here for the first time I attempted to specify just what those terms are and how we can use them to distinguish between good and bad works of history on film.

Historians and Film

Let's be blunt and admit it: historical films trouble and disturb professional historians—have troubled and disturbed historians for a long time. Listen to Louis Gottschalk of the University of Chicago, writing in 1935 to the president of Metro-Goldwyn-Mayer: "If the cinema art is going to draw its subjects so generously from history, it owes it to its patrons and its own higher ideals to achieve greater accuracy. No picture of a historical nature ought to be offered to the public until a reputable historian has had a chance to criticize and revise it."[1]

How can we think of this letter today? As touching? Naive? A window onto a simpler age that could actually conceive of Hollywood as having "higher ideals"? All of these? But if the attitude seems dated, the sentiments surely are not. Most historians today would be capable of saying, or thinking, the same thing. Give reputable scholars the chance to criticize and revise scripts, and we will surely have better history on the screen.

Question: Why do historians distrust the historical film? The overt answers: Films are inaccurate. They distort the past. They fictionalize, trivialize, and romanticize people, events, and movements. They falsify history.

The covert answers: Film is out of the control of historians. Film shows we do not own the past. Film creates a historical world with which books cannot compete, at least for popularity. Film is a disturbing symbol of an increasingly postliterate world (in which people can read but won't).

Impolite question: How many professional historians, when it comes to fields outside their areas of expertise, learn about the past from film? How many Americanists know the great Indian leader primarily from

Gandhi? Or Europeanists the American Civil War from *Glory,* or—horrors!—*Gone with the Wind?* Or Asianists early modern France from *The Return of Martin Guerre?*

Dislike (or fear) of the visual media has not prevented historians from becoming increasingly involved with film in recent years: film has invaded the classroom, though it is difficult to specify if this is due to the "laziness" of teachers, the postliteracy of students, or the realization that film can do something written words cannot. Scores, perhaps hundreds, of historians have become peripherally involved in the process of making films: some as advisers on film projects, dramatic and documentary, sponsored by the National Endowment for the Humanities (which requires that filmmakers create panels of advisers but—to disappoint Gottschalk—makes no provision that the advice actually be taken); others as talking heads in historical documentaries. Sessions on history and film have become a routine part of academic conferences (such as the one that gave birth to this book), as well as annual conventions of major professional groups like the Organization of American Historians and the American Historical Association. Reviews of historical films have become features of such academic journals as the *American Historical Review, Journal of American History, Radical History Review, Middle Eastern Studies Association Bulletin,* and *Latin American Research Review.*[2]

All this activity has hardly led to a consensus on how to evaluate the contribution of the "historical" film to "historical understanding." Nobody has yet begun to think systematically about what Hayden White has dubbed *historiophoty*—"the representation of history and our thought about it in visual images and filmic discourse."[3] In essays, books, and reviews, the historical film is dealt with piecemeal. Yet it is fair to say that two major approaches predominate.

The explicit approach takes motion pictures to be reflections of the social and political concerns of the era in which they were made. Typical is the anthology *American History/American Film,* which finds "history" in such works as *Rocky* (problems of blue-collar workers), *Invasion of the Body Snatchers* (conspiracy and conformity in the fifties), *Viva Zapata* (the cold war), and *Drums along the Mohawk* (persistence of American ideals).[4] This strategy insists that any film can be situated "historically." As indeed it can. But it also provides no specific role for the film that wants to talk about historical issues. Nor does it distinguish such a film from any other kind of film. Which leads to this question: Why not treat written works of history in the same way? They, too, reflect the concerns of the era in which they were made, yet we historians take their contents at face value and not simply as a reflection of something else. Why consider history books in terms of contents and historical films in terms of reflections? Is it that the screen itself only reflects images? That the analogy to Plato's cave is too close to allow us to trust what messages the shadows deliver?

The implicit approach essentially sees the motion

picture as a book transferred to the screen, subject to the same sorts of judgments about data, verifiability, argument, evidence, and logic that we use for written history. Involved here are two problematic assumptions: first, that the current practice of written history is the only possible way of understanding the relationship of past to present; and, second, that written history mirrors "reality." If the first of these assumptions is arguable, the second is not. Certainly by now we all know that history is never a mirror but a construction, congeries of data pulled together or "constituted" by some larger project or vision or theory that may not be articulated but is nonetheless embedded in the particular way history is practiced.

Let me put it another way: historians tend to use written works of history to critique visual history as if that written history were itself something solid and unproblematic. They have not treated written history as a mode of thought, a process, a particular way of using the traces of the past to make that past meaningful in the present.

The notion of history as constituted and problematic is hardly news to anyone familiar with current debates in criticism, but it needs to be stressed. For to talk about the failures and triumphs, strengths and weaknesses and possibilities of history on film, it is necessary to pull back the camera from a two-shot in which we see history on film and history on the page square off against each other, and to include in our new frame the larger realm of past and present in which both sorts of history are located and to which both refer. Seen this way, the question cannot be, Does the historical film convey facts or make arguments as well as written history? Rather, the appropriate questions are: What sort of historical world does each film construct and how does it construct that world? How can we make judgments about that construction? How and what does that historical construction mean to us? After these three questions are answered, we may wish to ask a fourth: How does the historical world on the screen relate to written history?

Varieties of Historical Film

We cannot talk about the historical "film" in the singular because the term covers a variety of ways of rendering the past on the screen. (Written history, too, comes in different subcategories—narrative, analytic, quantitative—but we have the notion that they all are part of some larger story about the past. Film seems more fragmented, perhaps because there exist no broad film histories of nations, eras, or civilizations that provide a historical framework for specific films.) It is possible to put history on film into a number of categories—history as drama, history as antidrama, history without heroes, history as spectacle, history as essay, personal history, oral history, postmodern history—but for heuristic purposes this essay will collapse all of these into three broad categories: history as drama, history as document, and history as experiment. Most of what follows will focus on history as drama, the most common form of historical film.

If you say "historical film," history as drama is probably what comes to mind. A staple of the screen ever since motion pictures began to tell stories, this form of film has been regularly produced all over the world—in the United States, France, Italy, Japan, China, Russia, India—wherever films are made. Some of the most beloved motion pictures have been dramatized history, or at least dramas set in the past. Among them are the kind of works that have given the historical film such a bad reputation—*Gone with the Wind, Cleopatra, The Private Life of Henry VIII.* It has been suggested by Natalie Davis that history as drama can be divided into two broad categories: films based on documentable persons or events or movements *(The Last Emperor, Gandhi, JFK)* and those whose central plot and characters are fictional, but whose historical setting is intrinsic to the story and meaning of the work *(Dangerous Liaisons, The Molly Maguires, Black Robe).*[5] But this distinction does not in fact have much explanatory power, for the categories quickly break down. A recent film, *Glory,* which I will analyze later in this essay, follows the common strategy of placing fictional characters next to historical characters in settings alternately documentable and wholly invented.

History as document is a more recent form than history as drama. Growing—at least in the United States—out of the social problem documentary of the thirties *(The Plow that Broke the Plains),* it was given a boost by the post-World War II patriotic retrospective *(Victory at Sea)*, and an even bigger boost by public money, which has been funneled by the National Endowment for the Humanities into historical films in the past two decades. In the most common form, a narrator (and/or historical witnesses or experts) speaks while we see recent footage of historical sites intercut with older footage, often from newsreels, along with photos, artifacts, paintings, graphics, newspaper and magazine clippings.

Professional historians trust history as document rather more than history as drama because it seems closer in spirit and practice to written history—seems both to deliver "facts" and to make some sort of traditional historical argument, whether as a feature *(The Wobblies, Huey Long, Statue of Liberty)* or as a series *(The Civil War, Eyes on the Prize)*. But a major problem for documentary lies precisely in the promise of its most obviously "historical" materials. All those old photographs and all that newsreel footage are saturated with a prepackaged emotion: nostalgia. The claim is that we can see (and, presumably, feel) what people in the past saw and felt. But that is hardly the case. For we can always see and feel much that the people in the photos and newsreels could not see: that their clothing and automobiles were old-fashioned, that their landscape lacked skyscrapers and other contemporary buildings, that their world was black and white (and haunting) and gone.

▾ ▾ ▾

History as experiment is an awkward term for a variety of filmic forms, both dramatic and documentary and sometimes a combination of the two. Included here are works made by avant-garde and independent filmmakers in the United States and Europe as well as in former communist countries and the Third World. Some of these films have become well known, even beloved (Sergei Eisenstein's *Oktober* and *Battleship Potemkin*, Roberto Rossellini's *The Rise of Louis XIV*). Some have achieved local or regional fame (*Ceddo* by Senegal's Ousmane Sembene, *Quilombo* by Brazil's Carlos Diegues). Others remain intellectual and cinematic cult films, more written about by theorists than seen by audiences (Alexander Kluge's *Die Patriotin*, Trinh T. Minh-ha's *Surname Viet Given Name Nam*, Alex Cox's *Walker*, Jill Godmilow's *Far from Poland*).

What these films have in common (apart from lack of exposure) is that all are made in opposition to the mainstream Hollywood film. Not just to the subject matter of Hollywood but to its way of constructing a world on the screen. All struggle in one or more ways against the codes of representation of the standard film. All refuse to see the screen as a transparent "window" onto a "realistic" world.

Why, you may ask, discuss such films? Why take time for works few people want to or can see? Because, as I have argued elsewhere, such works provide the possibility of what might be called a "serious" historical film, a historical film that parallels—but is very different from—the "serious" or scholarly written history, just as the standard Hollywood film parallels more popular, uncritical forms of written history, the kind history "buffs" like. At its best, history as experiment promises a revisioning of what we mean by the word *history*.

How Mainstream Films Construct a Historical World

The world that the standard or mainstream film constructs is, like the world we live in and the air we breathe, so familiar that we rarely think about how it is put together. That, of course, is the point. Films want to make us think they are reality. Yet the reality we see on the screen is neither inevitable nor somehow natural to the camera, but a vision creatively constructed out of bits and pieces of images taken from the surface of a world. Even if we know this already, we conveniently forget it in order to participate in the experience that cinema provides.

Less obvious is the fact that these bits and pieces are stuck together according to certain codes of representation, conventions of film that have been developed to create what may be called "cinematic realism"—a realism made up of certain kinds of shots in certain kinds of sequences seamlessly edited together and underscored by a sound track to give the viewer a sense that nothing (rather than everything) is being manipulated to create a world on screen in which we can all feel at home.

The reason to point to the codes of cinema (which have a vast literature of their own) is to emphasize the fundamental fiction that underlies the standard his-torical film—the notion that we can somehow look through the window of the screen directly at a "real" world, present or past. This "fiction" parallels a major convention of written history: its documentary or em-pirical element, which insists on the "reality" of the world it creates and analyzes. The written work of history, particularly the grand narrative, also attempts to put us into the world of the past, but our presence in a past created by words never seems as immediate as our presence in a past created on the screen.

History as drama and history as document are, in their standard forms, linked by this notion of the screen as a window onto a realistic world. It is true that the documentary—with its mixture of materials in differ-ent time zones, with its images of the past and its talking heads speaking in the present—often provides a window into two (or more) worlds. But those worlds share, both with each other and with history as drama, an identical structure and identical notions of document, chronology, cause, effect, and conse-quence. Which means that in talking about how the mainstream film creates its world, it is possible to make six points that apply equally to the dramatic film and the documentary.

1. The mainstream film tells history as a story, a tale with a beginning, middle, and an end. A tale that leaves you with a moral message and (usually) a feel-ing of uplift. A tale embedded in a larger view of

history that is always progressive, if sometimes Marxist (another form of progress).

To put it bluntly, no matter what the historical film, be the subject matter slavery, the Holocaust, or the Khmer Rouge, the message delivered on the screen is almost always that things are getting better or have gotten better or both. This is true of dramatic films *(Glory, Reds, The Last Emperor)* and true of documentaries *(The Civil War)*. It is also true (perhaps especially true) of radical documentaries like *The Wobblies, Seeing Red, The Good Fight,* and other hymns of praise to lost causes.

Often the message is not direct. A film about the horrors of the Holocaust or the failure of certain idealistic or radical movements may in fact seem to be a counterexample. But such works are always structured to leave us feeling: Aren't we lucky we did not live in those benighted times? Isn't it nice that certain people kept the flag of hope alive? Aren't we much better off today? Among those few films that leave a message of doubt about meaningful change or human progress, one might point to *Radio Bikini,* with its lingering questions about the possibility of controlling atomic energy or regaining an innocent faith in government, the military, or the scientific establishment. Or to *JFK,* with its worries about the future of American democracy, though the very fact that a big star like Kevin Costner, playing New Orleans attorney Jim Garrison, expresses these doubts tends to reassure us that the problems of the security state will be exposed.

▾ ▾ ▾

2. Film insists on history as the story of individuals, either men or women (but usually men) who are already renowned, or men and women who are made to seem important because they have been singled out by the camera and appear before us in such a large image on the screen. Those not already famous are common people who have done heroic or admirable things, or who have suffered unusually bad circumstances of exploitation and oppression. The point: both dramatic features and documentaries put individuals in the forefront of the historical process. Which means that the solution of their personal problems tends to substitute itself for the solution of historical problems. More accurately, the personal becomes a way of avoiding the often difficult or insoluble social problems pointed out by the film. In *The Last Emperor* the happiness of a single "reeducated" man stands for the entire Chinese people. In *Reds,* the final resolution of a stormy love affair between two Americans becomes a way of avoiding the contradictions of the Bolshevik Revolution. In *Radio Bikini,* the fate of a single sailor stands for all of those who were tainted with radiation from the atomic bomb tests of Operation Crossroads.

3. Film offers us history as the story of a closed, completed, and simple past. It provides no alternative possibilities to what we see happening on the screen, admits of no doubts, and promotes each historical assertion with the same degree of confidence. A subtle film like *The Return of Martin Guerre* may hint at hidden historical alternatives, at data not mentioned and sto-

ries untold, but such possibilities are never openly explored on the screen.

This confidence of the screen in its own assertions can trouble even historians who are sympathetic to the visual media. Natalie Davis, the historical consultant on the film, worries about the cost of the "powerful simplicity" of *Martin Guerre:* "Where was there room in this beautiful and compelling cinematographic recreation of a [sixteenth-century] village for the uncertainties, the 'perhapses,' the 'mayhavebeens' to which the historian has recourse when the evidence is inadequate or perplexing?"[6] Davis followed her work on the film by writing a book (with the same title) in order to restore this important dimension to the story of Martin Guerre. But anyone other than an expert viewing a historical film is confronted with a linear story that is unproblematic and uncontested in its view of what happened and why.

This is equally true of the documentary, despite the fact that it may call on various witnesses and experts who express alternative or opposing points of view. Through editing, these differences are never allowed to get out of hand or call into question the main theme of the work. The effect is much like that of dissenting minor characters in a drama, people whose opposing positions heighten the meaning of whatever tasks the heroes undertake. Ultimately, these alternative viewpoints make no real impact. They only serve to underline the truth and solidity of the main world or argument.

▼ ▼ ▼

4. Film emotionalizes, personalizes, and dramatizes history. Through actors and historical witnesses, it gives us history as triumph, anguish, joy, despair, adventure, suffering, and heroism. Both dramatized works and documentaries use the special capabilities of the medium—the closeup of the human face, the quick juxtaposition of disparate images, the power of music and sound effect—to heighten and intensify the feelings of the audience about the events depicted on the screen. (Written history is, of course, not devoid of emotion, but usually it points to emotion rather than inviting us to experience it. A historian has to be a very good writer to make us feel emotion while the poorest of filmmakers can easily touch our feelings.) Film thus raises the following issues: To what extent do we wish emotion to become a historical category? Part of historical understanding? Does history gain something by becoming empathic? Does film, in short, add to our understanding of the past by making us feel immediately and deeply about particular historical people, events, and situations?

5. Film so obviously gives us the "look" of the past—of buildings, landscapes, and artifacts—that we may not see what this does to our sense of history. So it is important to stress that more than simply the "look" of things, film provides a sense of how common objects appeared when they were in use. In film, period clothing does not hang limply on a dummy in a glass case, as it does in a museum; rather, it confines, emphasizes, and expresses the moving body. In film,

tools, utensils, weapons, and furniture are not items on display or images reproduced on the pages of books, but objects that people use and misuse, objects they depend upon and cherish, objects that can help to define their livelihoods, identities, lives, and destinies. This capability of film slides into what might be called false historicity. Or the myth of facticity, a mode on which Hollywood has long depended. This is the mistaken notion that mimesis is all, that history is in fact no more than a "period look," that things themselves *are* history, rather than *become* history because of what they mean to people of a particular time and place. The baleful Hollywood corollary: as long as you get the look right, you may freely invent characters and incidents and do whatever you want to the past to make it more interesting.

6. Film shows history as process. The world on the screen brings together things that, for analytic or structural purposes, written history often has to split apart. Economics, politics, race, class, and gender all come together in the lives and moments of individuals, groups, and nations. This characteristic of film throws into relief a certain convention—one might call it a "fiction"—of written history: the strategy that fractures the past into distinct chapters, topics, and categories; that treats gender in one chapter, race in another, economy in a third. Daniel Walkowitz points out that written history often compartmentalizes "the study of politics, family life, or social mobility." Film, by contrast, "provides an integrative image.

History in film becomes what it most centrally is: a process of changing social relationships where political and social questions—indeed, all aspects of the past, including the language used—are interwoven."[7] A character like Bertrande de Rols in *Martin Guerre* is at once a peasant, a woman, a wife, a property owner, a mother, a Catholic (but possibly a Protestant), a lover, a resident of Languedoc, a subject of Francis I of France.

How Experimental Films Construct a Historical World

The only collective way to characterize history as experiment is as films of opposition: opposition to mainstream practice, to Hollywood codes of "realism" and storytelling, to the kind of film described above. Certainly most experimental films will include some of the six characteristics of the standard film, but each will also attack or violate more than one of the mainstream conventions. Among films defined as history as experiment, it is possible to find the following: works that are analytic, unemotional, distanced, multicausal; historical worlds that are expressionist, surrealist, disjunctive, postmodern; histories that do not just show the past but also talk about how and what it means to the filmmaker (or to us) today.

How does history as experiment contest the characteristics of mainstream film? Here are some examples:
  1. History as a story set in the framework of (moral)

progress: the director Claude Lanzmann suggests in *Shoah* that the Holocaust was a product not of madness but of modernization, rationality, efficiency—that evil comes from progress. Alex Cox, in *Walker,* highlights the interpenetration of past and present and points to Manifest Destiny (with its assumptions of political and moral superiority and uplift) not as an impulse confined to pre-Civil War America but as a continuing part of our relationships with Central America.

2. History as a story of individuals: Soviet directors in the twenties, particularly Eisenstein in *Potemkin* and *Oktober,* created "collectivist" histories in which the mass is center stage and individuals emerge only briefly as momentary exemplars of larger trends (much as they do in written history). The same strategy has been pursued more recently by Latin American filmmakers (Jorge Sanjinés in *Power of the People,* Carlos Diegues in *Quilombo*).

3. History as a closed, uncontested story: Jill Godmilow in *Far from Poland* presents a "history" of the Solidarity movement through competing voices and images that refuse to resolve into a single story with a single meaning. Chris Marker in *Sans Soleil* and Trinh T. Minh-ha in *Surname Viet Given Name Nam* both dispense with story in favor of historical incident, pastiche, rumination, essay.

4. History as emotional, personal, dramatic: Roberto Rossellini made a series of sumptuously mounted but wholly dedramatized films, including *The Rise of Louis XIV* and *The Age of the Medici,* in which amateur actors

mouth lines rather than act them. The Brazilian Glauber Rocha achieves a similar Brechtian, distanced, unemotional past in such works as *Antonio das Mortes* and *Black God, White Devil*.

5. History with a "period look": Claude Lanzmann in *Shoah* tells a history of the Holocaust without a single historical image from the thirties or forties; everything was shot in the eighties, when the film was made. The same is largely true of Hans Jürgen Syberberg's *Hitler, a Film from Germany*, which re-creates the world of the Third Reich on a soundstage with puppets, parts of sets, props, actors, random historical objects, all illuminated by back-projected images.

6. History as process: the director Alexander Kluge in *Die Patriotin* creates history as a series of disjunctive images and data, a kind of collage or postmodern pastiche. Juan Downey in *Hard Times and Culture* uses a similar approach in a study of fin de siècle Vienna. Chris Marker in *Sans Soleil* envisions the past as made up of disconnected, synchronous, and erasable events.

History as experiment does not make the same claim on us as does the realist film. Rather than opening a window directly onto the past, it opens a window onto a different way of thinking about the past. The aim is not to tell everything, but to point to past events, or to converse about history, or to show why history should be meaningful to people in the present. Experimental films rarely sanitize, nationalize, or reify the past, though they often ideologize it. They tend to make bits and pieces of our historical experience accessible, sometimes in all its confusion. Such films rarely claim to be the only or the last word on their subject; many hope to make us think about the importance of a subject ignored by written history.

Experimental films may help to re-vision what we mean by history. Not tied to "realism," they bypass the demands for veracity, evidence, and argument that are a normal component of written history and go on to explore new and original ways of thinking about the past. Although such films are not popular, and although "reading" them can at first seem difficult for those who expect realism, their breakthroughs often are incorporated into the vocabulary of the mainstream film. The revolutionary montage effects of Eisenstein were long ago swallowed up by Hollywood. More recently, a German film, *The Nasty Girl*, uses a variety of avant-garde techniques (back projection rather than sets, composite shots, overtly absurdist elements) to portray the continuing desire of middle-class Germans to deny local complicity with the horrors of the Third Reich.

Reading and Judging the Historical Film

Our sense of the past is shaped and limited by the possibilities and practices of the medium in which that past is conveyed, be it the printed page, the spoken word, the painting, the photograph, or the moving image. Which means that whatever historical understanding the mainstream film can provide will be shaped and limited by the conventions of the closed story, the notion of progress, the emphasis on individuals, the single interpretation, the heightening of emotional states, the focus on surfaces.

These conventions mean that history on film will create a past different from the one provided by written history; indeed, they mean that history on film will always violate the norms of written history. To obtain the full benefits of the motion picture—dramatic story, character, look, emotional intensity, process—that is, to use film's power to the fullest, is to ensure alterations in the way we think of the past. The question then becomes: Do we learn anything worth learning by approaching the past through the conventions of the mainstream film (conventions that are, through the global influence of Hollywood, understood virtually everywhere in the world)?

A slight detour: it must always be remembered that history on film is not a discipline in which historians participate (to any great extent). It is a field whose standards historians may police but, with rare exceptions, only as onlookers. When we historians explore the historical film, it is history as practiced by others, which raises the ominous question: By what right do filmmakers speak of the past, by what right do they do history? The answer is liberating or frightening, depending on your point of view. Filmmakers speak of the past because, for whatever reasons—personal, artistic, political, monetary—they choose to speak. They speak the way historians did before the era of professional training in history, before history was a discipline. Today the historian speaks by virtue of this discipline, by virtue of special training and the standards of a profession. Filmmakers have no such standard training, and no common approach to history. Few, if any, devote more than a minor part of their careers to history; it is more likely that they are moved over the years to make one or two historical statements on film. (Though some major directors have devoted major parts of their careers to history, including Roberto Rossellini, Akira Kurosawa, Masahiro Shinoda, Carlos Diegues, Ousmane Sembene, and Oliver Stone.) One result: history on film will always be a more personal and quirky reflection on the meaning of the past than is the work of written history.

The haphazard nature of history on film and the lack of professional control make it all the more necessary that historians who care about public history learn how to "read" and "judge" film, learn how to mediate between the historical world of the filmmaker and that of the historian. This means that historians will have to reconsider the standards for history. Or learn to negotiate between our standards and those of filmmakers. We will have to adapt to film practice in order to criticize, to judge what is good and bad, to specify what can be learned from film about our relationship the past. The film world will not do this, for it has no ongoing stake in history (though some individual filmmakers do). The best we historians can hope for is that individual filmmakers will continue to create meaningful historical films that contribute to our understanding of the past. For only from studying how these films work can we begin to learn how to judge the historical film.

Among the many issues to face in learning how to judge the historical film, none is more important than the issue of invention. Central to understanding history as drama, this is the key issue. The most controversial. The one that sets history on film most apart from written history, which in principle eschews fiction (beyond the basic fiction that people, movements, and nations all live stories that are linear and moral). If we can find a way to accept and judge the inventions involved in any dramatic film, then we can accept lesser alterations—the omissions, the conflations—that make history on film so different from written history.

History as drama is shot through with fiction and invention from the smallest details to largest events. Take something simple, like the furnishings in a room where a historical personage sits—say Robert Gould Shaw, the chief character in *Glory*, a colonel and leader of the Fifty-fourth Massachusetts Regiment of black troops in the American Civil War. Or take some process, such as the training of the black volunteers who served under Shaw, or the reconstruction of the battles they fought. The room and the sequences are approximate rather than literal representations. They say this is more or less the way a room looked in 1862; these are the sorts of artifacts that might have been in such a room. This is more or less the way such soldiers trained, and the battles they fought must have looked something like this. The point: the camera's need to fill out the specifics of a particular historical scene, or to create a coherent (and moving) visual sequence, will always ensure large doses of invention in the historical film.

The same is true of character: all films will include fictional people or invented elements of character. The very use of an actor to "be" someone will always be a kind of fiction. If the person is "historical," the realistic film says what cannot truly be said: that this is how this person looked, moved, and sounded. If the individual has been created to exemplify a group of historical people (a worker during a strike, a shopkeeper during a revolution, a common soldier on a battlefield) a double fiction is involved: this is how this sort of person (whom we have created) looked, moved, and sounded. Both can obviously be no more than approximations of particular historical individuals, approximations that carry out some sense that we already have about how such people acted, moved, sounded, and behaved.

The same is true of incident: here invention is inevitable for a variety of reasons—to keep the story moving, to maintain intensity of feeling, to simplify complexity of events into plausible dramatic structure that will fit within filmic time constraints. Different kinds of fictional moves are involved here, moves we can label *Compression, Condensation, Alteration,* and *Metaphor.*

Consider this example: when Robert Gould Shaw

was offered command of the Fifty-fourth, he was in the field in Maryland, and he turned down the offer by letter. A couple of days later, urged by his abolitionist father, he changed his mind and accepted the position. To show the internal conflict expressed in this change within a dramatic context, *Glory* compresses Shaw's hesitation into a single scene at a party in Boston. The actor, Matthew Broderick, uses facial expression and body language to show Shaw's inner conflict. When he is offered the command by the governor of Massachusetts, he says something noncommittal and asks to be excused. There follows a scene with another officer, a kind of alter ego, an officer who voices Shaw's own unspoken doubts about the costs of taking such a command. These doubts register on Broderick's face, and we literally watch Shaw make this difficult decision, see that accepting the commission is a matter of conviction triumphing over fear. All of this scene, including the fellow officer, is invented, yet it is an invention that does no more than alter and compress the spirit of the documentable events into a particular dramatic form. In such a scene, film clearly does not reflect a truth—it creates one.

The difference between fiction and history is this: both tell stories, but the latter is a true story. Question: Need this be a "literal" truth, an exact copy of what took place in the past? Answer: In film, it can never be. And how about the printed page, is literal truth possible there? No. A description of a battle or a strike or a revolution is hardly a literal rendering of that series of events. Some sort of "fiction" or convention is involved here, one that allows a selection of evidence to stand for a larger historical experience, one that allows a small sampling of reports to represent the collective experience of thousands, tens of thousands, even millions who took part in or were affected by documentable events. One may call this convention Condensation too.

But isn't there a difference between *Condensation* and invention? Isn't creating character and incident different from condensing events? Is it not destructive of "history?" Not history on film. On the screen, history must be fictional in order to be true!

Why? Because filmic "literalism" is impossible. Yes, film may show us the world, or the surface of part of the world, but it can never provide a literal rendition of events that took place in the past. Can never be an exact replica of what happened (as if we knew exactly what happened). Of course, historical recounting has to be based on what literally happened, but the recounting itself can never be literal. Not on the screen and not, in fact, in the written word.

The word works differently from the image. The word can provide vast amounts of data in a small space. The word can generalize, talk of great abstractions like revolution, evolution, and progress, and make us believe that these things exist. (They do not, at least not as things, except upon the page.) To talk of such things is not to talk literally, but to talk in a symbolic or general way about the past. Film, with its need for a specific image, cannot make general statements about revolution or progress. Instead, film must summarize, synthesize, generalize, symbolize—in images. The best we can hope for is that historical data on film will be summarized with inventions and images that are apposite. Filmic generalizations will have to come through various techniques of condensation, synthesis, and symbolization. It is the historian's task to learn how to "read" this filmic historical vocabulary.

Clearly, we must read by new standards. What should they be? At the outset, we must accept that film cannot be seen as a window onto the past. What happens on screen can never be more than an approximation of what was said and done in the past; what happens on screen does not depict, but rather points to, the events of the past. This means that it is necessary for us to learn to judge the ways in which, through invention, film summarizes vast amounts of data or symbolizes complexities that otherwise could not be shown. We must recognize that film will always include images that are at once invented and true; true in that they symbolize, condense, or summarize larger amounts of data; true in that they impart an overall meaning of the past that can be verified, documented, or reasonably argued.

And how do we know what can be verified, documented, or reasonably argued? From the ongoing discourse of history; from the existing body of historical texts; from their data and arguments. Which is only to say that any "historical" film, like any work of written, graphic, or oral history, enters a body of preexisting knowledge and debate. To be considered "historical," rather than simply a costume drama that uses the past as an exotic setting for romance and adventure, a film must engage, directly or obliquely, the issues, ideas, data, and arguments of the ongoing discourse of history. Like the book, the historical film cannot exist in a state of historical innocence, cannot indulge in capricious invention, cannot ignore the findings and assertions and arguments of what we already know from other sources. Like any work of history, a film must be judged in terms of the knowledge of the past that we already possess. Like any work of history, it must situate itself within a body of other works, the ongoing (multimedia) debate over the importance of events and the meaning of the past.

False Invention/True Invention

Let me compare two films that invent freely as they depict historical events—*Mississippi Burning*, which uses "false" invention (ignores the discourse of history), and *Glory*, which uses "true" invention (engages the discourse of history).

Mississipi Burning (directed by Alan Parker, 1988) purports to depict the Freedom Summer of 1964, in the aftermath of the killing of three civil rights workers, two white and one black. Taking for its heroes two FBI men, the film marginalizes blacks and insists that though they are victims of racism, they in fact had little to do with their own voting rights drive. The resulting message is that the government protected African-Americans and played a major role in the voter registration drive of Freedom Summer. Yet this is palpably untrue. This story simply excludes too much of what we already know about Mississippi Freedom Summer and the rather belated actions of the FBI to solve the murder of the three civil rights workers.[8] The central message of that summer, as responsible historians have shown, was not simply that blacks were oppressed, but that they worked as a community to alleviate their own oppression. This is the theme that the film chooses to ignore. By focusing on the actions of fictional FBI agents, the film engages in "false" invention and must be judged as bad history. Indeed, by marginalizing African-Americans in the story of their own struggle, the film seems to reinforce the racism it ostensibly combats.

Glory (directed by Edward Zwick, 1989) is as inventive as *Mississippi Burning*, but its inventions engage the historical discourse surrounding the film's subject: the Fifty-fourth Massachusetts Regiment commanded by Robert Gould Shaw, and, by implication, the larger story of African-American volunteers in the American Civil War. Here are examples of how specific strategies of invention work in *Glory*.

Alteration. Most of the soldiers in the Fifty-fourth were not, as the film implies, ex-slaves, but in fact had been freemen before the war. One can justify this alteration by suggesting that it serves to bring the particular experience of this unit into line with the larger experience of African-Americans in the Civil War, to generalize from the Fifty-fourth to what happened elsewhere in the Union to slaves who were freed.

Compression. Rather than creating characters from regimental histories, the film focuses on four main African-American characters, each of whom is a stereotype—the country boy, the wise older man, the angry black nationalist, the Northern intellectual. The filmic reason is obviously dramatic: such diverse individuals create a range of possibilities for tension and conflict that will reveal character and change. The historical reason is that these four men stand for the various possible positions that blacks could take toward the Civil War and the larger issues of racism and black-white relations, topics that are not solely "historical"— or that, like all historical topics, involve an interpenetration of past and present.

Invention. Although there is no record of this happening, in the film the quartermaster of the division to which the Fifty-fourth belongs refuses to give boots to the black troops. His ostensible reason is that the regiment will not be used in battle, but the real reason is that he does not like African-Americans or think them capable of fighting. Clearly, this incident is one of many ways the film points to the kinds of Northern racism that black soldiers faced. Another way of showing the racism might have been by cutting to the antiblack draft riots in New York, but such a strategy could vitiate the intensity of the film and the experience of our main characters. This incident is an invention of something that could well have happened; it is the invention of a truth.

Metaphor. Robert Gould Shaw is shown practicing cavalry charges by slicing off the tops of watermelons affixed to poles. Did the historical Shaw practice this way? Does it matter? The meaning of the metaphor is obvious and apropos.

Question: Does using a white officer as a main character violate the historical experience of these African-American volunteers? Answer: No, it provides a different experience, a broader experience. Even if the decision to have a white main character was in part made for box office reasons (as it surely must have been), the film provides another explanation. Throughout *Glory* we see and hear Robert Gould Shaw saying (in voice-over extracts from actual letters) that though he admires them, he cannot comprehend the culture of these men he leads. The clear implication is that we too will never fully understand their life. We viewers, in other words, stand outside the experience we are viewing just as Shaw does. Which suggests that film itself can only approximate that lost historical life. We do not understand the life of the soldiers because we are always distant spectators of the experience of the past, which we may glimpse but never fully understand.

For all its inventions, *Glory* does not violate the discourse of history, what we know about the overall experience of the men of the Fifty-fourth Regiment— their military activities, their attitudes, and those of others toward them.[9] At the same time, the film clearly adds to our understanding of the Fifty-fourth

Regiment through a sense of immediacy and intimacy, through empathic feelings and that special quality of shared experience that the film conveys so well. To share the up-close danger of Civil War battles as rendered on the screen, for example, is to appreciate and understand the possibilities of bravery in a new way.[10]

There is no doubt that the film simplifies, generalizes, even stereotypes. But it proposes nothing that clashes with the "truth" of the Fifty-fourth Regiment or the other black military units that fought for the Union—that men volunteered, trained under difficult conditions, and gave their lives in part to achieve a certain sense of manhood for themselves and pride for their people. Only the moral may be suspect: when the bodies of the white officer and one of his black men (the angriest, the one most suspicious of whites, the one who refuses to carry the flag, the one who has been whipped by this same officer) are pitched into a ditch and fall almost into an embrace, the implication seems to be that the Fifty-fourth Massachusetts Regiment and the Civil War solved the problem of race in America. How much more interesting, how much truer, might have been an image that suggested that the problems of race were to continue to be central to the national experience.

A New Kind of History

Of all the elements that make up a historical film, fiction, or invention, has to be the most problematic (for historians). To accept invention is, of course, to change significantly the way we think about history. It is to alter one of written history's basic elements: its documentary or empirical aspect. To take history on film seriously is to accept the notion that the empirical is but one way of thinking about the meaning of the past.

Accepting the changes in history that mainstream film proposes is not to collapse all standards of historical truth, but to accept another way of understanding our relationship to the past, another way of pursuing that conversation about where we came from, where we are going, and who we are. Film neither replaces written history nor supplements it. Film stands adjacent to written history, as it does to other forms of dealing with the past such as memory and the oral tradition.

What, after all, are the alternatives? To try to enforce Gottschalk's dicta? To insist that historians begin to make films that are absolutely accurate, absolutely true (as if this were possible) to the reality of the past? Not only is this impossible for financial reasons, but when historians do make "accurate" films (witness *The Adams Chronicles*), they tend to be dull as both film and history, for they do not make use of the full visual and dramatic power of the medium. A second alternative: history as experiment. But whatever new insights into the past experimental films provide, they tend to give up large audiences. A final alternative: to wish film away, to ignore film as history. But this would be to surrender the larger sense of history to others, many of whom may only wish to profit from the past. Worse yet, it would be to deny ourselves the potential of this powerful medium to express the meaning of the past.

It is time for the historian to accept the mainstream historical film as a new kind of history that, like all history, operates within certain limited boundaries. As a different endeavor from written history, film certainly cannot be judged by the same standards. Film creates a world of history that stands adjacent to written and oral history; the exact location of the understanding and meaning it provides cannot yet be specified.

We must begin to think of history on film as closer to past forms of history, as a way of dealing with the past that is more like oral history, or history told by bards, or *griots* in Africa, or history contained in classic epics. Perhaps film is a postliterate equivalent of the preliterate way of dealing with the past, of those forms of history in which scientific, documentary accuracy was not yet a consideration, forms in which any notion of fact was of less importance than the sound of a voice, the rhythm of a line, the magic of words. One can have similar aesthetic moments in film, when objects or scenes are included simply for their look, the sheer visual pleasure they impart. Such elements may well detract from the documentary aspect, yet they add something as well, even if we do not yet know how to evaluate that "something."

The major difference between the present and the

preliterate world, however obvious, must be under-scored: literacy has intervened. This means that however poetic or expressive it may be, history on film enters into a world where "scientific" and documentary history have long been pursued and are still undertaken, where accuracy of event and detail has its own lengthy tradition. This tradition, in a sense, raises history on film to a new level, for it provides a check on what can be invented and expressed. To be taken seriously, the historical film must not violate the overall data and meanings of what we already know of the past. All changes and inventions must be apposite to the truths of that discourse, and judgment must emerge from the accumulated knowledge of the world of historical texts into which the film enters.

II
The Historical Film

▼ ▼ ▼

· 3 ·

Reds as History

Reds provided me fifteen minutes of fame. After the film's release, I had the pleasure of being misquoted in a number of mass circulation publications. The program committee of the American Historical Association asked me to set up a screening during the annual convention, and I can still see the scene before the show, three hundred historians in the lobby of the Motion Picture Academy of Arts and Sciences, munching on stale pastries provided by the publicity department of Paramount Pictures, whose members evidently worried that the film itself might be hard to swallow. Of the (too) many pieces I wrote on the film, this is by far the most substantial. As the earliest piece in this volume, it stands as a testament to traditional thinking, a work of mild outrage by an academic who may suspect but has not yet quite learned that a film can never be a book.

I must begin this essay on a personal note. At the conclusion of *Reds* my name appears in the credits as historical consultant. Since on this side of the Atlantic it may seem unusual to criticize a work in which one has taken part (in France nobody blinked an eye when the playful Roland Barthes reviewed his own book), I wish to be quite specific about my role in the production of the film. Beginning in 1972 (three years before my book, *Romantic Revolutionary: A Biography of John Reed,* was first published),[1] Warren Beatty and I talked a few times a year about the film on John Reed that he was always just about to make. Our conversations dealt with Reed, Louise Bryant, their friends and associates, and the historical era in which they lived. In 1979, when shooting was about to begin, we formalized our association with a contract. The talks continued, not only with Beatty, but with others involved in the production. I also read various versions of the screenplay and offered criticism and suggestions (some taken, some rejected), both historical and dramatic. During shooting, I was occasionally asked specific questions about such things as the number of delegates to the Socialist party convention in 1919, or the contents of Bryant's and Reed's letters when they were separated. In the spring of 1980 I spent some time with the film company on location in Spain.

A major disappointment was that Beatty politely but firmly refused my generous offer to play the role of Trotsky in the film. Trotsky has, I have always thought, the best single line of the entire Russian Revolution. From the podium of the ballroom in Smolny Institute on November 7, 1917, he looks down "with a pale, cruel face" (John Reed's description) and thunders at those opponents of the Bolsheviks who are withdrawing from the meeting in protest, "They are just so much refuse which will be swept into the garbage-heap of history!" One might equally well use this phrase to describe what most historical films do to their unwitting subjects. In what follows, I wish to examine to what extent John Reed and his associates have suffered such a fate.

I

The title is uncompromising, bold, and forthright. Once the prerelease jokes about catering to a drug subculture or Cincinnati baseball fans are put aside, once the wry comparisons to that other sharp, four-letter title, *Jaws,* are cleared away, there is no hiding the basic fact: this is a film about radicals and revolutionaries, about people who take upon themselves an appellation despised in America, people unafraid to call themselves Communists. Yet, as the advertisements have shown and the reviews have underscored, *Reds* is a love story. But it is a particular love story set in a particular historical period among a particular set of people. By choosing the United States, by taking as his main characters John Reed and Louise Bryant and recreating aspects of the subculture in which they lived, by overtly confronting the origins of the American Communist party and the first, stormy days of the Comintern, and framing the film with a series of historical witnesses who lived through that period, Beatty has chosen to make a historical statement. To see *Reds* as only a love story is to accept a kind of one-dimensionality, to ignore the very real influence of motion pictures on our lives.

This denial of responsibility should not go uncontested. *Reds* is important not merely because of that well-noted irony—$33 million, perhaps more, to tell the story of a revolutionary and founder of the Communist Labor Party—but because it is one of those rare Hollywood films that deals with the subject of native radicalism. How odd this seems. In certain quarters a myth persists of a "Red Decade" in Hollywood. Congressional committees in the forties and fifties rather enjoyed investigating the "Communist influence" in Hollywood. One result was the jailing of ten unfriendly witnesses for contempt of Congress; another was a blacklist which kept hundreds of people from working at their trade for many years. Yet the objective record shows how unwarranted were right-wing fears of subversion in Hollywood. Judged by the contents of films, there was no "Red Decade." Radicals there were in the film industry, but their politics rarely made it to the screen except in the most oblique fashion. The House Un-American Activities Committee had to be content with lines like "Share and share alike, that's democracy" as baleful examples of Communist influence.

Consider this: only once before *Reds* has a Hollywood film chronicled the life of a historical American radical. It took a Swedish director to make a film about Joe Hill, the organizer and songwriter for the Industrial Workers of the World who died at the hands of a firing squad in Utah, and an Italian company to tell the story of Sacco and Vanzetti, the anarchists whose Massachusetts death sentences were such a cause célèbre in the twenties. Until now, the only compara-

ble production has been *Bound for Glory* (1977), a work
based upon the life of the folksinger Woody Guthrie.
(For some reason, Hollywood has done better with
foreign radicals, especially Mexican. Whatever their
artistic merits, *Viva Villa* and *Viva Zapata* do deal with
revolutionaries.) Unlike *Reds, Bound for Glory* waffles
about its hero's political connections, ignores his relationship to the Communist Party, and never mentions
his weekly column in the *People's World* (the West
Coast Communist Party newspaper). Guthrie comes
across as a man of the people, the balladeer of dust-
bowl migrants who suffer from ecological disaster and
exploitation at the hands of large landowners. His
forebears are as much cinematic as historical, for in its
message the film is a kind of *Grapes of Wrath* revisited.
Guthrie's views seem a combination of those of Tom
Joad in his final speech ("Wherever there's a cop
beatin' up a guy, I'll be there") and of the Preacher
Casey, whose mystical vision of radical togetherness is
much closer to Emerson's concept of the oversoul
than to Marx's dialectics.

This has been typical of the Hollywood approach to
radicalism. The thirties brought forth a number of
films in which common people were downtrodden
and oppressed by rich businessmen or bankers—usually played by portly Edward Arnold, who seemed to
have dollar signs on his tiepin—but never did a real
radical lead a revolt. Instead, any revolutionary thrust
dissolved into a sentimental insistence upon the Christian virtues of "little people" banding together, caring
for one another, indulging in brotherly love, and hop-

ing for the future. Frank Capra was the master of the genre; his *Meet John Doe* and *Mr. Smith Goes to Washington* were morality plays in which Evil, no matter how powerful, managed to defeat itself by the end of the third reel. Sixties radicalism on film was more sophisticated about the staying power of evil, but equally defensive in stance. Rather than focusing on specific institutions, radical anger was diffused into a generalized hatred for an entire "sick society." The apolitical protagonist of *Easy Rider* became a hero, and his arbitrary death at the hands of rednecks—like the brutal manhandling by police of the virtuous undergraduates of *Strawberry Statement*—was transformed into a symbol of the Left's ultimate impotence.

Compared to all this, *Reds* is an audacious undertaking. It is the first Hollywood film to make a hero of a Communist, the first to suggest the existence of a bohemian-radical subculture during the second decade of the century, the first to hint at the bitter issues that shattered world radical movements at the time of the Russian Revolution, and certainly the first to have an all-American couple bed down to the stirring strains of the "Internationale." For an American public generally ignorant of, and either indifferent or hostile to, the whole notion of radicalism, it is bound to provide an image—perhaps the only image—of what the native Left is all about. This means that the film's historical contents must be taken seriously, and makes it worthwhile to explore just what *Reds* is saying about American radicalism, the history of our century, and—not so incidentally—the nature of history itself.

II

To analyze *Reds* as history, one must begin with its most obviously historical device, the Witnesses. The film is framed by the comments of elderly men and women who were Reed's contemporaries, and their recollections provide its historical backbone. From them we learn of bohemian pranks in Greenwich Village, of free love and affairs, and who was sleeping with whom. They describe the radicalism of the Industrial Workers of the World, the antiwar movement in the United States, the coming of the Russian Revolution, the Allied attempts to strangle bolshevism, and the repression of dissent at home. Most important, they recall the relationship of Jack Reed and Louise Bryant, and reflect philosophically on the meaning of their turbulent lives.

Judged by reviews, the use of the Witnesses is one of the most successful aspects of the film. The only recurrent criticism concerns the failure to identify them with name tags. It has been suggested that this was an aesthetic decision, a desire not to make the film seem too much like a documentary. Perhaps. But the overall thrust of *Reds* suggests a deeper reason. To name the Witnesses would be to make them individually more accountable for what they say. As it is, they have the effect of a latter-day Greek chorus, one which creates the conditions of a world in which the leading characters play out their destiny. Keeping them anonymous is a technique calculated to impress and lull the audience; never can the viewer be certain exactly which remarks on politics, sex, art, or the main characters fit together. We are left with the powerful feeling that the Witnesses were there, they remember these events; they lived through those turbulent times and survived to tell their tales, to reflect upon history. Collectively, they are worthy teachers, voices of the past speaking in tones at once personal and impersonal, subjective and objective.

When Beatty in our very first conversation outlined the idea of putting Reed's contemporaries onto film, I thought it a brilliant stroke. I still do. But something happened in the execution that transformed an apparently historical device into a profoundly ahistorical one. Beyond the fact that most of the Witnesses did not actually know Bryant and Reed (another reason for keeping their identities vague) lies the troubling implication of the way their remarks are used. Sometimes the Witnesses are an impressive bunch—winning, humorous, informative, and often forceful as they present alternate versions of the same events. But often they are vague, forgetful, and self-contradictory.

For people mostly in their eighties this is natural enough, except that in this case, they—or more specifically, their memories—are being used as the historical framework of a film. (Much has been made in reviews of the fifteen years of research supposedly undertaken by Beatty. In fact, there is nothing in *Reds* which cannot easily be found in histories of the period and biographies of Reed and his friends.) For those who care about history, here is the locus of the problem. In *Reds,* memory is equated with history. Memory is seen as faulty, and thus history is as well. This approach allows the filmmaker to have it both ways. He can at once indulge himself by playing historian and yet ignore—whenever convenient—all known techniques of assessing evidence from the past, as well as the findings of previous research and scholarship. To put it more directly: the Witnesses ultimately suggest that nobody can know the truth about Reed and Bryant. Thus the filmmaker can tell us whatever story he wishes (and history be damned!).

III

Let us take this violation of the very basis of history as given, and go on to see just what story *Reds* chooses to tell. My focus will be Reed because however much one insists that the film has two principals, it never would have been made had he not achieved journalistic fame, written *Ten Days That Shook the World,* and died a left-wing martyr. Nor, I may add, did the notion of Bryant and Reed as equals and of their love story as central enter the first seven years of my conversations with Beatty. In fact, this was never voiced until production was under way.

From the first moments of the film it is obvious that John Reed is a man who holds unconventional opinions and does unconventional things. He describes the war in Europe—this is 1915, two years before American entry—as being fought for "profits." On their first meeting he delivers a night-long lecture to Bryant on the connection between capitalism and war (a good

Progressive might have done the same). He casually asks Louise, a married woman, to come and live with him. In New York he is part of a lively group of people who reside in Greenwich Village. Most of their time is spent eating, drinking, and partying, except for those late night moments when they listen to Emma Goldman—whose radical edge occasionally disappears into a motherly concern over a good cup of coffee—warn of the imminent dangers of American involvement in the war.

Eventually it becomes clear that this unconventionality must be radicalism. Reed listens to stories of dreadful conditions among factory workers (who for some reason are gathered in a barn), nods approval to Big Bill Haywood's militant appeals for the IWW, defends the workers in a fracas with police and gets knocked down. He breaks with an apparently liberal editor who trims his articles ("Nobody edits my stuff") and says he will publish in the *Masses*. He leaves a Provincetown summer vacation to cover the 1916 Democratic Convention and returns to bore his friends with a all-night lecture on politics. When he learns Louise is having an affair with Eugene O'Neill, he ignores, in the name of personal freedom, what more bourgeois folk would consider a betrayal. When the United States enters the conflict in April 1917, he bravely takes the platform at a mass meeting to announce "This is not my war," and briefly lands in jail. A Socialist tells him that great things are happening in Russia and, blocked from his vocation as a journalist by his antiwar opinions, he journeys there, arrives on the eve of the October Revolution, makes a speech of solidarity with the Russian workers, and in the excitement of the great ten days is reborn as a Bolshevik.

Almost all these events are more or less historically accurate. Liberties are often taken with time and place: Reed certainly did not know in 1916 of Louise's affair with O'Neill (he got wind of it when they separated in the spring of 1917); he married her not because of jealousy of O'Neill, but because he faced that dangerous kidney operation and wanted her to be his legal heir; he did not use the marvelous line "Class struggle sure plays hell with your poetry" in 1916, but in 1919 while organizing the Communist Labor Party; he did not go to France to meet Louise in 1917 (she returned to the United States); and certainly they could not have ridden a train from France to Russia in September 1917 without waving away many millions of Allied and German troops (they went by boat from New York to Norway).

Such quibbles aside, one can assert that to this point—and indeed in the second half as well, following the Bolshevik takeover of Russia—the film does manage to capture the overall pattern of Reed's life. But only the surface. Underneath the events on screen something crucial is missing, something called motivation. Nowhere does *Reds* really come to grips with or satisfactorily explain just why this privileged Harvard graduate from a stuffy, upperclass Portland background takes a journey so far along a radical path. Such a question may never trouble moviegoers content that a hero only be committed to defending some sort of ideals. But certainly it is crucial for understanding not only history, but the actions that take place on screen.

To explain Reed's trajectory from Portland through Harvard and Greenwich Village to a grave at the base of the Kremlin Wall, to make sense of his beliefs and death, it is necessary to comprehend the era and milieu in which he lived—not through fallible memories, but through history, which does not fuzz the issues of social change. Reed was a hero for the subculture of bohemians, artists, and radicals that between 1910 and 1920 had its headquarters in the Village, outposts in other American cities, and ties both emotional and personal to similar centers across the Atlantic. This role, achieved through a combination of talent, real literary accomplishment, and bravado, was given a kind of official status in 1914 when Walter Lippmann published a *New Republic* article entitled "Legendary John Reed." The burden of the piece—alternately admiring, caustic, and witty—was that just five years out of Harvard, Reed was already larger than life, a man who poured himself into one enthusiasm after another—travel, love affairs, labor strikes, modern art, poetry, being jailed. Others took his actions more seriously. Fifty years later Louis Untermeyer, a coeditor on the *Masses*, recalled him as "an idealist who combined boisterous humor and a quiet passion for truth . . . Jack remains in my mind as the most vivid figure of the period" (*RR*, p. 6).

As a hero-figure, Reed embodied and expressed the values and ideals of a subculture. In the decade after

1910, he was surrounded in the Village, Province-town, and Croton by people from the first large generation of middle class Americans to wrestle seriously with doctrines that had developed in Europe over the course of a century. The intellectual demands on his associates were enormous. Raised as children of late Victorian America, a society whose intellectual boundaries were capitalism, the Constitution, Christianity, and genteel culture, they confronted an immense variety of new social and artistic visions: the works of Marx, Freud, Bergson, and Nietzsche; the politics of anarchism, syndicalism, socialism, and industrial unionism; the visual modernism of cubists, futurists, and fauves; the shocking writings of Strindberg, Dostoyevsky, and D. H. Lawrence; the attractive and disturbing world views implied by feminism and free love.

Unlike some of their European counterparts, these artists and intellectuals exhibited few signs of morbidity or fears of decadence. Bohemia in the United States was too new and playful for such attitudes; besides, they were good enough Americans to believe in progress, to expect a better future, one in which their divergent visions would blend into some marvelous new reality. Too easily they spoke the word "revolution," without much idea of what it might mean beyond a wide-ranging liberation in the realms of art, lifestyle, economics, politics, and sexual relationships. To jumble together such diverse spheres was also a national habit. It was an era when the custodians of American culture—editors, critics, professors, art collectors—saw themselves as protecting a kind of castle, threatened at once by the vulgarity of the newly rich and the alien standards of recent immigrants. At the time of the Armory Show in 1913, the *New York Times* equated the cubists with bomb-throwing anarchists. No wonder radicals greeted an attack on any rampart as an assault on the entire old bourgeois order.

The shortcomings of *Reds* in depicting this Bohemia lie less in what it shows than in what it ignores, less in doctrines voiced than in the important connections it fails to make. A multidimensional, vibrant, creative, radical bohemian subculture is at once flattened and polarized. Reed's friends hang about bars and restaurants, cavort on the beach, don silly costumes, dance a lot, and perform amateurish theatricals. When not with them, Jack is busy sounding off against editors, politicians, police, capitalists, profiteers, and the war (later this extends to right-wing socialists, the AFL, and Communist party members). Nowhere does *Reds* connect these extremes or indicate that while the Village folk were certainly capable of having fun, they were dead serious about art, politics, and social change, that if they played with life, they also struggled painfully toward new artistic and intellectual visions in works and deeds that have left an enduring legacy. Merely to name Reed's friends and associates is to chronicle an important era in American cultural life: Max Eastman, Randolph Bourne, Waldo Frank, Floyd Dell, Edna St. Vincent Millay, Alan Seeger, Crystal Eastman, Susan Glaspell, George Cram Cook, John Sloan, George Bellows, George Luks, Jo Davidson,

Robert Minor, Marsden Hartley, Robert Edmund Jones, Eugene O'Neill, Margaret Sanger.

More extreme in behavior than his contemporaries, Reed was at one with this subculture; anxious for great change on all fronts, although vague before 1917 about how it might occur. He arrived in the Village in 1911 with two incompatible desires: to become a great poet and to make a million dollars. At first journalism merely paid his bills, then the vivid reports of Pancho Villa's revolution that appeared in *Metropolitan Magazine* in 1914 made him famous. Yet this success did not extend to serious poetry and fiction (he had no trouble selling light, topical verse and slick stories). His best short stories were naturalistic slices which, like the paintings of the Ashcan school, simultaneously celebrated and criticized the seamy underside of urban life, the world of hookers, cops, con men, and ward-heel politicians. These were rejected by the editors of family publications as being "immoral." It was the need for an outlet for this fiction, rather than any political motive, which first drew him to the *Masses.* Then he was swept into the whirlwind of Village life.

Later Reed claimed that "Ideas alone did not mean much to me . . . It didn't come to me from books that the workers produced all the wealth of the world, which went to those who did not earn it" (*RR,* p. 111). But the social and intellectual context in which he lived did help to create a structure of connections between the plight of others and his own situation. Theory joined the contradictions of a commercial culture that Reed experienced (the incompatible demands of self-expression and the genteel, literary marketplace) with the contradictions of factory labor (the promise of economic freedom and the reality of inescapable wage slavery). The writer, he came to see, was like the common laborer; he could be hired when needed and fired when what he produced was no longer acceptable to editors or publishers. From there it was but a short step to acceptance of the idea that the World War was also caused by a demand for profits, and that those benefiting economically from the conflict were the same people who wished to squelch change in social and cultural matters.

The war brought personal and political issues to a head. For Reed and his contemporaries, Europe was the much admired cradle both of high culture and of radical movements. With the major powers locked in a struggle that appeared to be destroying "civilization" (including the Socialist International), one reaction was to ignore the war and hold aloft the torch of cultural and intellectual life in the United States. Reed's response was more personal and more complicated. His best writing had been elicited by labor struggles at Paterson and Ludlow, then in early 1914 the experience with Pancho Villa's troops touched his prose for the first time with a tinge of greatness. In the autumn he journeyed to the Western Front and found a senseless slaughter that was excused by patriotic slogans voiced with cynicism by politicians and received with contempt by the troops themselves. That his Village background led him to judge the conflict "A Trader's War" is not surprising, but his critique had a deeply personal component. The meaningless enormity of the European conflict made it difficult to write well; in fact, he could hardly write at all. For Reed, the artist, the problems of the world out there had now become his own. The antiwar struggle that he waged in the following four years was intimately connected to his struggle to write well—or as he put it, to have something worth writing about.

After 1914 Reed may be seen as a man in search of a subject to match his radical beliefs and artistic powers. By 1917 he was growing discouraged. The civilization he had seen "change and broaden and sweeten" in the years before 1914 was now gone in the "red blast of war." The proletariat, which some doctrinaire minds expected to stop the conflict through revolution, seemed hopelessly divided, blind to its class interest. In the spring of 1917 he wrote sadly, "I am not sure any more that the working class is capable of revolution" (*RR*, p. 270). Then came the journey to Petrograd, the drama of the great ten days, the incarnation of revolutionary visions in the flesh of Lenin, Trotsky, and the great mass of Russian workers and soldiers. The artist and the radical in Reed caught fire. Now he had a subject worthy of engaging his pen and his deepest beliefs. No wonder his first lengthy article on the revolution reeked with hope phrased in quasi-religious terms: "This proletarian government will last . . . in history, a pillar of fire for mankind forever" (*RR*, p. 301).

This faith sustained him through the final three years of his life. It carried him through sedition trials and police harassment in the United States in 1918–1919, fired him to complete *Ten Days That Shook the World* in two months, buoyed him up during the discouraging schisms and endlessly dull meetings (*Reds* mostly depicts the fiery confrontations) that marked the birth of two Communist parties in the United States. It helps to explain the limitations of Louise's resounding (and apparently telling) speech that in 1919 he had become a power seeker and was returning to Russia to represent "thirty men in a basement." The answer to this is given later in the film when Reed suggests to Emma Goldman that if she gives up on the revolution, her life will have had no meaning. Here he is obviously thinking of himself.

If Reed's faith seems unwarranted in the film, that may be due to a too narrow focus on politics. Jack, in fact, never gave up on art (in his Finnish prison cell he was sketching notes for two novels). At home, war propaganda and repression had shattered Bohemia. Friends like the onetime pacifist Floyd Dell had joined the army, while the anarchist George Bellows had gone from drawing anticapitalist cartoons to creating prowar posters. But in Russia the revolution had apparently unleashed a huge burst of artistic creativity. In 1919–1920, Reed met Mayakovsky and his circle of poets, and some of the artists whose startling abstractions were changing the rules of visual art. Such experimentation, encouraged by Commissar Lunacharsky and tolerated by Lenin, seemed final proof of the Village idea that political, economic, and artistic change went together. No wonder Reed endured the abuse of Zinoviev and the repeated defeats over the labor issue at the Second Congress of the Communist International. The workers' state was also a state for artists. It seemed a dream come true.

IV

Reed's crucial internal struggles are only hinted at during *Reds*. Of the commitment to bolshevism, Max Eastman can say, "With him it's a religion," and in an important scene Louise may confront him with the notion "You're an artist, Jack." But the hints in these remarks are never developed. Yet to say that the work does not depict Reed's conflict over belief and art may be to belabor the obvious. *Reds* is not meant to be a psychological drama, but an interpersonal one, set against the movement of great historical events. The focus is clearly on Jack and Louise, on their stormy romance, breakups, and reconciliations, on the inherent conflict of two-career households, the meaning of fidelity in an age of liberation, on the problematics of any relationship between men and women once the confining strictures of the bourgeois nuclear family are left behind.

Some debate has already arisen over the film's portrait of the relationship. There seems to be general agreement that Louise is the more interesting of the two main characters—after all, she grows, struggles, and changes, whereas Jack is virtually the same in the last frame as in the first. But the extent to which *Reds* may be a feminist statement or merely another sophisticated reassertion of male supremacy is open to dispute. Advocates of the former position may see signs of Bryant's strength and independence in the affair with O'Neill, her job as a correspondent in France, her demand that she and Reed go to Russia as a nonsexual team, her refusal to sanction his 1919 trip back to Moscow, and in Reed's deathbed recognition that they are "comrades." Opponents may stress her early lack of direction in Greenwich Village, the affair with O'Neill, the jealousy over Reed's affairs, her sexual capitulation during the ten days, and the final journey to his side as an indication that this is business as usual between Hollywood men and women.

That the historical Louise was intelligent, talented, and attractive is true; that she and Jack quarrelled over careers is likely, and over affairs, certain; that she left him to work in France in 1917 and deplored his return to Russia is accurate; that he loved her from the first week they met and was deeply devoted—in his fashion—to her right to the end is attested to in many letters and personal documents. But, as if fearing that only worldly accomplishment can make people love one another, *Reds* consistently inflates the historic importance of Louise and diminishes that of Jack. It accepts her untrue claim that she wrote for the *Portland Oregonian* before they met; it neglects to mention that Reed obtained for her the job with the Wheeler syndicate for the trip to Europe; it fails to show that during the separation each was miserable without the other, and that she happily returned to him in New York; it suggests that during the Russian Revolution they were artistic equals, when a most casual reading of their works will show that Louise was no more than a competent reporter in the presence of a great story and Jack a major journalist at the height of his powers; it shows Louise testifying to a Senate subcommittee, but fails to indicate that Reed spent a good deal of time at the same witness table and outspokenly proclaimed, "I have always advocated a revolution in the United States" (*RR*, p. 344). Nor does the film give any indication that he stood trial for sedition with the other editors of the *Masses*.

The final section of the film, Reed's imprisonment in Finland and Bryant's dramatic journey toward reconciliation, contains more fancy than fact. To suggest that Reed was escaping the Comintern is to ignore that when arrested in Finland (in the hold of a ship, not on a hand-propelled rail car) he was carrying more than $15,000 in diamonds and currency to help finance the Communist party at home. During his confinement, communication did pass between the two, and only when Jack, after his release, cabled that he was returning to Moscow did Louise leave the United States to join him. Her motives were more complex than the loving altruism portrayed in *Reds*. During Reed's absence Louise had been living in Woodstock, New York, with the painter Andrew Dasburg. From shipboard—she did not stow away, but journeyed openly, with Hearst press credentials—she wrote Dasburg that the reason for going was to keep Reed from coming home, where he would no doubt be jailed for sedition. Of his possible return, she said,

"It would destroy us—you can see that. It would destroy all three" (p. 380, *RR*).

No doubt the crossing into Russia contained elements of danger, but neither fears of frostbite nor of a
broken leg from skiing could have plagued Louise,
who entered the country in August. And no, that
scene on the station platform did not really take place.
Before leaving for Baku on August 25, Reed had received a telegram saying that Louise would be in Moscow on his return. On September 25, he ran into her
hotel room and they spent a pleasant ten days together before he grew ill with typhus. During that
final loving period, it is unlikely that Jack told her of
the young Russian woman who had warmed his bed
during their long separation.

V

Like any work of art, *Reds* is more than the sum of its
parts. For all its omissions, errors, and shortcomings,
the film contains far more serious historical data than
almost any other Hollywood effort. In the first American motion picture to show a Communist as a decent
human being, Beatty's John Reed is a nice guy, generally moral and upright, with a winsome touch of
naivete. His forebears seem literary and fictional. Reed
on screen is related to that old American type, the
frontiersman, to Natty Bumppo and his latter-day incarnation, John Wayne. Strong and active in the
world of men, he is occasionally boyish, shy, and in-
articulate with women (this despite his extensive sex-

ual experience, always hinted at rather than shown). Reed makes radicalism acceptable by being a kind of left-wing Archie Bunker. That is, Bunker is a lovable bigot, Reed a lovable Commie. (Before its opening, Beatty took the film to the White House. President Reagan's reported comment on the work was favorable, though he was evidently upset at the unhappy ending.)

Friends on the political Left have hailed *Reds* as a significant departure for Hollywood. Publications like the *Nation* and the *Progressive* have given the film good reviews, and the newspaper *In These Times* has claimed it "makes socialism sexy." No doubt. How nice to have as a hero a genuine, historic radical. But here is a marvelous irony. So desperate is the Left for media heroes that it may wink at violations of its own, usually ignored, history. For years radicals have exposed the ideology of free enterprise, and in intellectual circles a cottage industry has grown up that applies Antonio Gramsci's powerful notion of cultural hegemony to a variety of historical situations. Yet what is *Reds* but a flowering example of hegemony in full bloom?

Let me be specific here. *Reds* is no outright piece of fiction but a subtle restructuring of history. It humanizes a radical hero by domesticating him, putting his love life at center stage. (In Reed's case this is particularly problematic, for in his single autobiographical effort, written only for himself, he devotes only a couple of sentences in thirty pages to all his lovers, including Louise.) It plays with the issues of radicalism and revolution just enough to make them serious, but certainly not enough to inform the public as to what they really are. Nor does it so much as hint that the underlying conflict of the real John Reed—which was not the struggle between love and revolution, but between the demands of an ambitious self and those of a market economy—still very much exists today.

In fact, what better example can we have of this dilemma than *Reds* itself? An immensely rich and popular star worries for a decade before making a film about a radical. When he does, the story is told within the confines of filmic conventions that detract from the basic vision of his hero. Politics and art take a back seat to love. Thus we have all that cute situation-comedy shtick: the puppy that runs upstairs every time Jack and Louise are in bed; Reed cooking dinner and spilling everything, or hitting his head repeatedly on the lamp in Petrograd, or telling a joke that amuses no one (a bit left over from *McCabe and Mrs. Miller*). Thus we have the Zhivago-like trek and the tearjerking reunion. To argue, as some may, that this is necessary for a big-budget film and a mass audience is only to prove the point. From its length, subject matter, and approach, it appears that Beatty wished to made a bid for immortality, to create a great, serious work like *Citizen Kane*. His inability to do so speaks volumes about the hegemony of commercial values.

In no way am I accusing Beatty of cowardice. My argument is simply that he, too, is trapped by the conventions and standards of our culture (which include the box office but are not exclusively monetary). Once in my presence Beatty said something like "Nobody knows what history really is." Naively I took this to be a sophisticated statement about the multiplicity of interpretations inherent in any historical situation. I was wrong. What it represented was a fascination with history and a fear of its power to judge us. No wonder the film exhibits a deep ambivalence toward its main subject. No wonder it is necessary both to domesticate John Reed and occasionally to make him a bit of a buffoon. To take Reed's life and death seriously would be to see one's own commercial ventures for what they are, to recognize without deception that while a brave undertaking, *Reds* panders to popular prejudices and expectations and thus avoids the risk that serious art must take. John Reed would, I think, understand the problems with *Reds*, but he might not be inclined to forgive them.

This harsh judgment is not directed at the filmmaker alone. Beatty has done a real service. He has given us a radical hero and more radical history than has ever before been shown in an American film. If the film is popular among a wide spectrum of people, perhaps it is in part because we all want to be a bit radical, and yet well off and comfortable, venturesome and yet safe. So did John Reed. But for him there came a time when contradictory desires could no longer be held together. Trapped by his own beliefs, Reed's deepest responses led to a militant antiwar stance, growing disillusionment with his homeland, and to death as a Soviet hero. He was a man who knew the taste of comfort and fame, but who ultimately found it less savory than that of truth.

The controlling metaphor of *Reds* is that of Reed chasing a military wagon that he never quite catches. This is our first and only glimpse of him in Mexico, and it is repeated in Russia just before the final reunion with Louise. In the shooting—as in history—Beatty/Reed made it onto the wagon in Russia; in Mexico, no such incident occurred. To me, the scene is unconsciously self-referential, a statement more about *Reds* than about its subject. In reality, Reed found his wagon, his cause, his revolution. Once he did so, neither love, nor the desire to write, nor fears that bureaucracy was beginning to sour the revolution could make him back down on his commitment.

The filmmaker is more ambivalent about his own accomplishment. John Reed's story is Warren Beatty's wagon; he chased it for over a decade and even with the completion of *Reds* does not seem to have caught it. One way to understand this is by returning to the roots of our culture, to Thomas Jefferson's prophetic insight that ours is a social order dedicated to the pursuit (rather than the attainment?) of happiness. This notion runs athwart the religious truths of our tradition, the notion that external happiness is an epiphenomenon, that real happiness can only grow inside ourselves ("the Kingdom of God is within"). Accepting this older truth may affect our worldly pursuits and entail a loss of the fame and fortune that good Americans—movie stars above all—are taught to equate with being loved. The dilemma, then, is not merely that of Warren Beatty or John Reed. In the profoundest sense, the problems with *Reds* as history are very much our own.

· 4 ·

The Good Fight

History, Memory, Documentary

The following essay was originally delivered as part of a day-long symposium at the Smithsonian Institution in Washington, D.C. held in December 1986 to commemorate the fiftieth anniversary of the Spanish Civil War. My role was to introduce and then, after a screening, to comment upon The Good Fight, *a feature-length documentary about the Americans who fought as volunteers under the banner of the Lincoln Battalion of the International Brigades. The battalion was the subject of my first book,* Crusade of the Left: The Lincoln Battalion in the Spanish Civil War. *I had served as an advisor on the film project and, when money ran out, had volunteered to write the narration for the film. I decided not simply to celebrate what the filmmakers had done but to point to some of the limitations and problematics of the form they had used, the standard documentary of talking heads and archival footage. This was only the second piece I had written on film and history and it betrays the marks of a Dragnet historian who is beginning to struggle with theoretical issues of how film works to (re)create the past.*

This film is a hard act to follow. Especially with words. I have come to know this very well because, at a number of events this year celebrating the fiftieth anniversary of the Spanish Civil War and the Lincoln Brigade, I have had the honor of talking after a screening of *The Good Fight*. On each occasion words have seemed terribly superfluous and almost wholly irrelevant to the remembered and emotional experience of Spain that we have shared for the past hour and a half with these veterans of the conflict. And when, as today, there are veterans present, I grow even more sensitive to the uneasy fit between language and the visual image, between memory and history, between what we say and what we do.

At the outset, then, I want it to be known that in the very deepest sense I admire and honor the men who fought in Spain and the filmmakers who gave four years of their creative lives to conceptualizing, financing, and producing this motion picture. Both groups have been and are, given the context of their times, brave, dedicated, and talented in many ways; both have affected how we think about the past, and, especially, the Spanish Civil War. But (and you knew there was a "but" coming) as a historian who has written on the Lincoln Battalion; and as one who is committed to certain standards for written history, standards that prevent one from concealing data or ignoring unwelcome issues or turning the complex into something overly simple; and as one who is deeply concerned about representations of history in the visual media, I take it as my task today not just to praise *The Good Fight* but to raise some questions about the way it deals with history.

Like all interesting attempts to represent the past, this film implicitly raises a number of broad questions: Why do history? Why do this particular history? What is the point of this work of history? Such questions may seem to take us away from Spain, but they are necessary if we are to understand what sort of history is presented in the film. My contention is that the aims of our histories tend to govern what we find in the past and how we represent it. (This is true both for academic historians and for filmmakers, but historians work in a professional context which delimits their aims; or, rather, makes them all accept similar, positivist aims for representing the past, while filmmakers are freer to set personal agendas for history.) Looked at in this way, we must judge *The Good Fight* to be history as homage—homage to a certain kind of commitment and to a tradition of activism, one in which the filmmakers clearly situate themselves. This desire to do homage is hardly a neutral factor. It underlies the aesthetic decisions that shape the film and helps to provide its structure, meaning, and message.

The makers of the film did not start out—as I did when a graduate student in 1963 working on my dissertation on the Lincoln Battalion—finding everything they possibly could about Americans in Spain and then shaping it into a critical historical narrative. They did not—as I did—turn up some things about the Lincoln Battalion that they did not like but which had to be included anyway, because some notion of truth was more important than any notion of homage. (Besides, I had a doctoral committee looking over my shoulder and had to justify what I wrote.) And yet it would be a mistake to say that they consciously ignored or buried unpleasant data or findings. What the filmmakers did, instead, was to act in accordance with the codes of a profession other than history; they made decisions, that is, as filmmakers, not historians. Like all historians faced with too much data, they had to be highly selective in the material used. And they tended to make decisions on the basis not of some notion of written truth but of a filmic truth (or belief, or ideology), one which asserts that anything that cannot be explained in images, or which slows the relentless filmic pace of twenty-four frames a second, will destroy some larger truth by boring or losing the audience.

Holding your attention—that, above all, constitutes the truth of the filmmaker and that is where his or her chief effort goes. So after reading up on Spain and the Lincolns, and after talking to some academic experts (insisted upon, anyway, by the terms of the NEH grant), and getting a sense of the broad outlines of their story, the makers of *The Good Fight* went looking for veterans to put on the screen. They knew the kinds of people they were looking for. By now you know them too—and not just in this film but in all such films. Talking heads in a documentary must have photogenic faces and interesting voices, and be a fund of good stories, alive on camera, and full of that ineffable quality we call charisma. (They must, in short, have some of that quality we associate with Hollywood stars—and thus none of us is surprised to learn that

Bill Bailey has played a role in a major feature film.) For this sort of documentary they must, like American Army units in World War II movies, also be representative of the population at large, rather than of the brigade (which in this case means highly unrepresentative samples of blacks and women).

Any traditional historian is bound to have problems with a work that is put together in this way, but before mentioning some of them, let me specify what the film does well. Certainly *The Good Fight* puts flesh and blood into history. It introduces us to a group of compelling individuals and lets us hear their firsthand stories about the thirties and the Spanish Civil War, thus humanizing what might be no more than a series of deadly abstractions that we find in some historical accounts. (Film by its nature always deals in specific images, never generalities: that is part of its strong impact upon us.) The film argues a thesis about the need for political commitment and its efficacy; it shows that battles which seem to be lost may, in fact, later be won; it affirms a faith in life and the continuity of struggles for social justice by its movement from "We were there" to "We are here" to "We shall be there." Finally, it provides an introduction to the history of a topic long ignored by our schools and media. To step outside the film to its social role, one can suggest that *The Good Fight* has no doubt introduced lots of people to its subject. Thus it has been and will continue to be a vehicle of education.

Despite these virtues, *The Good Fight* suffers from a number of real problems in the eyes of a historian who works in words. They are, incidentally, problems that mark virtually all historical documentaries of this sort (such as *The Wobblies,* or *Seeing Red,* or to deal with the other side of the political spectrum, the award-winning *Huey Long*), problems apparently endemic to films which depend upon talking heads to structure the past, and then use historical footage to illustrate their words. Indeed, because of its coherent story, high production qualities, and excellent editing, *The Good Fight* is, I believe, among the best of such films. So to investigate its shortcomings is, in part, to deal with the shortcomings of an entire genre.

Here are some of the things that the film fails to do: It makes assertions about but does not really analyze the politics of Depression America. It barely touches upon the complexities of Spanish politics, especially the great and often fatal differences among parties supporting the Popular Front. It stays almost entirely within the framework of memory, which means it uses narration only grudgingly, and largely to set the stage for its characters. It makes little use of contemporary—that is, nineteen-thirties—documents to say how things felt to volunteers at the time, and relies exclusively upon what they remember about the war more than forty years later. It presents a cross-section of volunteers without giving any real data about what sorts of people in the aggregate volunteered for Spain; in other words it completely avoids any broadscale socioeconomic or psychological factors underlying such decisions. It depicts to some extent what the Americans thought of Spain, but never bothers with the reverse question beyond the most superficial level, namely, What did the Spanish think of the Americans and other foreign volunteers? It wholly avoids the important issues of desertion, discipline, labor battalions, or even the extent—very little, as my research shows—to which the anti-Trotsky terrorism of the Stalin purges spilled over into the ranks of the Americans.

The Good Fight fails to do these things for three basic reasons: (1) because the format of talking heads privileges memory (and nostalgia) rather than history; (2) because the film never asks questions of its witnesses, never comments upon their opinions, however wrong or inaccurate they may be; (3) because the filmmakers refuse to take up any topic, no matter how important, that might slow down the film and thus possibly bore the audience. Indeed, this latter attitude in a sense explains the previous two points. By allowing the witnesses to say what they wish to say not just about their own experiences but about matters of fact, and by not ever questioning their veracity or reliability, the film ensures greater sympathy for them as characters. This means that a number of the historical problems of the film flow from the ideology of the well-made documentary, which is not so much different from the ideology of the well-made Hollywood film. (It also may mean that the filmmakers suffer from the simplistic belief that the past can speak, unmediated, for itself.)

Let me exemplify what I have said with a specific example. One of my fears from early on in planning the film was that the complex politics of Spain, and of the Left, would be overly simplified or ignored. I also thought it especially important that the film include at least something about the issues of desertion and discipline, and that the allied issue of possible Stalinist terrorism in the ranks be raised, even if only to deny that it existed among the Americans. Though repeatedly promising to handle the issue, the directors never did. My final attempt to make them do so came when I was writing the narration. (This was done, incidentally, only after the images were in place; narration for the film was a kind of afterthought, added only when it became apparent that the whole story could not be told simply with the voices of veterans.) At that late point I was openly overruled on the following grounds: the directors could find no visual images to illustrate the issue and were adamant that the film not become static with too much talk; and the topic was too complex to handle quickly, and the film—like all films—had so much good footage that it was already in danger of running too long. This decision to sacrifice complexity to action underlines a convention of the genre: the documentary bows to a double tyranny—which is to say, an ideology—of the necessary image and perpetual movement. And woe be to those elements of history which can neither be illustrated nor quickly summarized.

This criticism is not meant harshly. As I have already said, I think *The Good Fight* is an excellent exemplar of a certain kind of documentary. But this kind of work must not be mistaken for critical history, and cannot be judged by the standards of written history. It is a visual sort of history—it is history as homage. The strength of this sort of work is not analysis or theory, not the combining of detail into a powerful, logical argument, but the evocation of emotion, the etching of individual character, the magic ability of verbal and visual memory to bring an earlier world and earlier selves into the present, where they can be experienced, shared, and even admired. Certainly nobody could deny that *The Good Fight* makes us feel the strength and passion of the commitment that took people to Spain, and allows us to see that such commitment can create enough meaning to last a lifetime.

And yet because this film is so good, there is something in me that longs for more from it—that longs for some greater intellectual content, greater regard for the complexities of history, greater self-awareness on the part of the filmmakers that they are not recording history but creating it. I would like the film to recognize, for example, that the relationship between the voice-overs of the veterans and the stock images of Spain is problematic, or constructed, not direct. I would like the film to question the simple sweetness of the stories its heroes are telling; to complexify them as human beings; to, occasionally, pin them to the wall when necessary and point up the failings, weaknesses, and doubts that make them like the rest of us. I would like the film to explore the political issues in their complexity, rather than flattening them into, essentially, guys in white hats and guys in black hats (among the former there were many shades of white).

I would like, finally, *The Good Fight* to admit its own limitations. To admit that it is only an introduction to a history of the Lincoln Brigade.

How can such things be done on film? Well, they can and have been. Since the sixties, filmmakers—the most obvious being Jean-Luc Godard—have found ways of making films that refuse to provide a satisfying, linear story with a good emotional release at the end. (Indeed, the radicals among them will claim that such a release is an inherent part of a reactionary art form that does no more than reconcile people to an unjust social order.) While I cannot detail the way such a history might be done, let me suggest some possibilities. One might have a narration that does not attempt omniscience, but which raises questions, even calls itself into question. Or asks you to question it, saying something like this: "Listen. Don't believe that you are getting the real history, the complete history from this motion picture. History is much more complex than documentaries, including this one, make it out to be. We're talking about millions of people making decisions—how can we possibly give it to you in ninety minutes? Or even ninety hours? People have spent their lives studying this issue, so how could all their knowledge and ideas get boiled down into such a short time? In this film we are giving you something distilled by three people born long after the events and not trained systematically in history. Our motives are pure and we have worked on this bloody film for six years and have almost gone broke to get it done. But you had best not confuse our labor of love with historical accuracy. If this topic interests you—and we think it should—go out and read some books on the topic [these could even be listed]. In that way you will begin to have some insight into all the events and issues that we could not include in this film. And you will begin to learn something, rather than just feel the retrospective emotions, of the Abraham Lincoln Brigade and the Spanish Civil War."

Such a statement in a documentary would be a very radical act. (It has been done, by the way; go see Jill Godmilow's film, *Far from Poland*, a subtle and daring "history" of Solidarity.) Like all radical acts, it would mean taking a risk—the filmmakers' taking the risk of losing an audience conditioned by Hollywood aesthetics, an audience which, in general, prefers nostalgia to history and emotion to thought. Let me not be mistaken here: I do not wish to decry the emotional catharsis that film can provide, but neither do I wish to mistake it for something other than it is. *The Good Fight* is a marvelous addition to the literature on the Lincoln Brigade, but its truths—like those of most films—are aimed at the heart rather than the mind.

· 5 ·

JFK

Historical Fact/Historical Film

In 1989 the American Historical Review *asked me to create an annual section devoted to film reviews. Some historians objected to this intrusion of the fictions associated with the visual media into a world of historical scholarship, but in general the section has been popular, especially among younger members of the profession. So popular that in 1993 the big film of the year,* JFK, *was snatched away from me and made the subject of a special forum. While other scholars used the film as the basis of essays about Kennedy, Oswald, homophobia in America (and the usual suspects), I focused on the issue of genre—how* JFK *worked as a piece of history within the conventions of the mainstream dramatic film.*

To those of us interested in historical films, the fuss in the media over *JFK* feels familiar. Complaints that the film bends and twists history; accusations that the director Oliver Stone willfully mixes fact and fiction, fails to delineate clearly between evidence and speculation, creates characters who never existed and incidents which never occurred—these are the sorts of charges that are made every time a historical film on a sensitive subject appears. With *JFK*, the controversy is particularly heated because of both the topic and its treatment. The film hits us with a double whammy: one of America's most popular directors not only explores our recent history's most touchy subject, but does so in a bravura motion picture that (maybe it's a triple whammy) also takes a highly critical stance toward major branches of the American government.

Complaints over the misuse of history in film seem to be based upon two notions: first, that a historical film is no more than a piece of written history transferred to the screen, and thus subject to the same rules of historical practice; and second, that a fact is a fact and that history is little more than an organized compilation of such facts. We who write history should find these assertions questionable. At least we have to be aware that "facts" never stand alone, but are always called forth (or constituted) by the work in which they then become embedded. This means that in order to evaluate the way in which any work of history—including a motion picture—uses facts (or data) to evoke the past, we must investigate the aims, forms, and possibilities of the historical project in which that data appears.

All this is to say something simple but important: a film is not a book. To judge the contribution of a work like *JFK*, we must try to understand just what a historical film can do.

As a dramatic motion picture, *JFK* comes to us in a form that has been virtually unexplored by people interested in the study of past events. Neither historians nor anyone else have given much thought to the most basic questions about the possibilities and standards of history when it is represented in the visual media. Evaluations of historical films in essays and reviews are always made on an individual basis. Certainly the historical profession has no agreed-upon way to answer any of the following questions: What kind of historical knowledge or understanding can a historical film provide? How can we situate it in relation to written history? What are its responsibilities to the historical "fact"? What can it tell us about the past that the written word cannot?

Such questions are too broad to answer here, but they are good to keep in mind as we think about *JFK*. My aim in what follows here is less to deal with the contributions and shortcomings of the film than to approach it as part of a tradition. I want to situate *JFK* as both a certain kind of film and a certain kind of historical film. Placed in this context, the factual "errors" (if one wants to term them that) of the work will appear to be less the fault of the filmmaker than a condition of both the medium and the kind of movie he has chosen to make. The contributions (if one wants to call them that) of the film, on the other hand, are in large measure its own—they derive less from the form of the film than from the way that form has been put to use.

There is no single way to do history on film. The traditional division into the dramatic work and the documentary is increasingly irrelevant as recent films (*JFK* included) often blur the distinction between the two. My own research has suggested that history on film comes in a number of different forms. *JFK*, despite the many documentary-type elements that it contains, belongs to what is certainly the most popular type of film, the Hollywood—or mainstream—drama. This sort of film is marked, as cinema scholars have shown, by a number of characteristics, the chief being its desire to make us believe in that what we see in the theater is true. To this end, the mainstream film utilizes a specific sort of film language, a self-effacing, seamless language of shot, editing, and sound designed to make the screen seem no more than a window onto unmediated "reality."

Along with "realism," four other elements are crucial to an understanding the mainstream historical film:

- Hollywood history is delivered in a story with beginning, middle, and end—a story that has a moral message, and one that is usually embodied in a progressive view of history.
- The story is closed, completed, and ultimately, simple. Alternative versions of the past are not shown; the *Rashomon* approach is never used in such works.
- History is a story of individuals—usually heroic individuals who do unusual things for the good of others, if not all humankind (ultimately, the audience).
- Historical issues are personalized, emotionalized, and dramatized—for film appeals to our feelings as a way of adding to our knowledge or affecting our beliefs.

Such elements go a long way toward explaining the shape of *JFK*. The story is not that of President Kennedy but of Jim Garrison, the heroic, embattled, uncorruptible investigator who wishes to make sense of JFK's assassination and its apparent coverup, not just for himself but for his country and its traditions—that is, for the audience, for us. More than almost any other historical film, this one swamps us with data—some of it, in the black-and-white flashbacks that illustrate the stages of the investigation, tentative or contradictory (so much is thrown at us that, on a single viewing, the viewer has difficulty absorbing all the details of events discussed and shown). Yet even if contradictions do exist, the main line of the story is closed and completed, and the moral message is clear: the assassination was the result of conspiracy that involved agencies and officials of the U.S. government; the aim of the assassination was to get rid of a president who wished to curb the military and end the Cold War; and the "fascist" elements responsible for the assassination and the subsequent coverup are a clear and ongoing threat to what little is left of American democracy.

Let me put it simply: if the conventions of the mainstream historical film make it difficult for such works to create a past that stays within the norms by which we judge written history, certain other factors make it impossible. It is not just that most of the data by which we know the past come from the realm of words and that the filmmaker is always involved in a good deal of translation from one medium to another, attempting to find a visual equivalent for written evidence. It is also that the mainstream historical film is shot through with fiction or invention from smallest of details to largest events. (Historians do not, of course, approve of fiction, aside from the underlying fiction that the past itself can be truly told in neat, linear stories.)

Invention occurs for at least two reasons: the requirements of dramatic structure, and the need of the camera to fill out the specifics of historical scenes. Drama demands the invention of incidents and characters because historical events rarely occur with the kind of shape, order, and intensity that will keep an audience in its seats. Inventions are used for a variety of reasons: to keep the story moving, to keep emotions high, to simplify complex events into a plausible structure that will fit within filmic time constraints. When the screenplay of *JFK* creates a fascist, homosexual prisoner named Willie O'Keefe to give Garrison evidence that Clay Shaw was involved with Oswald, or invents a Deep Throat character (Donald Sutherland) in Washington to help Garrison make sense of all the evidence he has gathered by providing a theory to hold it all together, one has the sense that Oliver Stone is doing no more than finding a plausible, dramatic way of summarizing evidence that comes from too many sources to depict on the screen.

Invention due to the demands of the camera may be a subtler factor, but it is no less significant in shaping the historical film. Consider, for example, something as simple as the furnishings in a room where a historical character sits—say, Jim Garrison's office or conference room, or Clay Shaw's apartment. Or think of the clothing that characters wear, or the words they speak. All such elements have to be approximate rather than literal representations. They say: this is more or less the way Garrison's room looked in 1966, or these are the kinds of clothes a character might well have worn, or these are likely examples of the words he or she spoke.

The same is true of individuals. This is not just a matter of the director's making up characters. Even historical people become largely fictional on the screen. The very use of an actor to portray someone is itself a kind of fiction. If the person is an actual historical figure such as Garrison, and even if the actor looks like the figure (which is not true in *JFK*, for the actor Kevin Costner looks little like the real Garrison, who in turn does not look much like Earl Warren, the character he portrays), the film on a literal level says what cannot truly be said: not just that this is how the person looked, but also that this is how he moved, walked, and gestured, and this is how he sounded when he spoke.

Settings and clothing, the look and sound of characters—to analyze a historical film is to see how small fictions like this shade into larger and larger inventions. Yet even the tiniest sorts of fictions are not unimportant factors. At least not if history is about the meaning of past events. In a medium where visual evidence is crucial to understanding, such pervasive fictions are major contributors to the meaning of the film, including its historical meaning. So, too, is that elusive, extra-historical element, the aura carried by famous actors and actresses. A star like Kevin Costner, fresh from his award-winning *Dances with Wolves,* cannot simply disappear into the character of Garrison. From his previous film he carries for many in the audience a strong feeling of the decent, simple, honest American, the war hero man who more than a century ago was critical of a certain kind of expansionist militarism in American life.

Like a history book, a historical film—despite Hollywood's desire for "realism"—is not a window onto the past but a construction of a past; like a history book, a film handles evidence from that past within a certain framework of possibilities and a tradition of practice. For neither the writer of history nor the director of a film is historical literalism a possibility. No matter how literal-minded a director might be, film cannot do more than point to the events of the past; at best, film can approximate historic moments, the things that were once said and done, but it cannot replicate them. Like the book, film will use evidence to create historical works, but this evidence will always be a highly reduced or concentrated sample; given its limited screentime, the film will never provide more than a fraction of the empirical data of an article on the same topic. Even as a lengthy three-hour film which includes an unusually dense barrage of information, *JFK* must often make major points with sparse evidence or invented images. Within the world of the film, the idea that Kennedy was ready to withdraw American troops from Viet Nam, for example, rests on the mention of a single memorandum and the testimony of a fictional character. The notion that

Black Americans loved Kennedy is conveyed by having a single woman say "He did so much for this country, for colored people."

What I am suggesting is this: the Hollywood historical film will always include images that are at once invented and yet may still be considered true; true in that they symbolize, condense, or summarize larger amounts of data; true in that they carry out the overall meaning of the past which can be verified, documented, or reasonably argued. But, one may ask, how do we know what can be verified, documented, or reasonably argued? That is, how do we know whether Kennedy was about to withdraw troops or whether he was loved by African-Americans? Both of these highly debatable points must be answered from outside the film, from the ongoing discourse of history—the existing body of historical texts, their data and arguments. This need for outside verification is not unique to film. Any work about the past, be it a piece of written, visual, or oral history, enters a body of pre-existing knowledge and debate. To be considered "historical," rather than simply a costume drama that uses the past as an exotic setting for romance and adventure, a film must engage the issues, ideas, data, and arguments of that ongoing discourse. Whatever else it does or does not do, *JFK* certainly meets these requirements as a work of history.

The practice of written history is not a single kind of practice. And if that practice is dependent upon data, its value and contribution has never been wholly a matter of that data and their accuracy. Certainly different works of history use data in different ways make different sorts of contributions to our understanding. Some works of history may be chiefly important for the data they create and deliver. Some for their evocation of people and events of a vanished time and place. Some for their elegance of argument or skill at representation. Some for raising new questions about the past, or for raising old questions for a new generation.

It is the same with historical films. They come in different forms and they undertake different historical tasks. Some evoke the past, bringing it to life, making us intensely feel people, places, and moments long gone—this surely is one of the glories of the motion picture. (Who can sit through *JFK* without reliving many of the agonies of the sixties which it depicts?) But film may do more than evoke: the historical film can be a provocation to thought and intervention into history, a way of revisioning the past. We don't go to the Hollywood historical film for data but for drama: for the way it intensifies the issues of the past, for the way it shows us the world as process, makes us participate in the confusion, multiplicities, and complexities of events long gone.

JFK is a film that takes up more than one historical burden. Because it chooses as its central strategy an investigation of the past, the film has a self-reflexive edge, one which suggests much about the difficulty of any historical undertaking and the near impossibility of arriving at definitive historical truths. More important, perhaps, *JFK* makes an apparently old issue come to life—indeed, the reaction it has evoked makes it seem like a very successful piece of historical work. Not a work that tells us the truth about the past, but one that questions the official truths about the past so provocatively that we are forced once again to look to history and consider how events mean to us today. Like a good historian, Stone begins *JFK* with a preface that contains a thesis; he uses Dwight Eisenhower's farewell address, with its warning about the possible effect of the military industrial complex on the future of our country, to set the stage for a film that will illustrate the prescience of Ike's words. By doing this, Stone forces us to face the kind of larger issue that a more sober historian, mired in tons of data and worried about the judgments of professional colleagues, might find difficult to raise so sharply: Has something gone wrong with America since the sixties?

Oliver Stone has been faulted for thinking that many changes in the United States stem from the killing of a single president, but others who are less sanguine about the judgments and actions of Kennedy may take him as a symbol—certainly the experience of the film, like that of any important work of history, resonates well beyond the ideas of its creator and speaks to and for those who do not share Stone's strong faith in JFK. When assessing *JFK*, one should ask this question: Who else in America has dared to raise such historical issues so powerfully (or at all) in a popular medium? If it is part of the burden of the historical work to make us rethink how we got to where we are, and to make us question values that we and our leaders and our nation live by, then whatever its flaws, *JFK* has to be among the most important works of American history ever to appear on the screen.

· 6 ·

Walker

The Dramatic Film as (Postmodern) History

Walker *had a double importance for me. By outrageously flouting the conventions of the mainstream historical film, it underlined clearly what those conventions were. And at the same time, it pointed beyond those conventions toward a history on film that was at once more complex and critical than what we usually see on the big screen. So strong was the impact of the film that it sent me back to read everything substantial published on William Walker, in both English and Spanish, since his invasion of Nicaragua in 1854. This is the kind of research that more historians who write on film should undertake. Not only does it demonstrate how each age fulfills its particular ideological and psychic needs in the past, it also suggests—if one is open to visual language—how film can be a superb medium for rendering the past as complex, multidimensional, and intellectually challenging. Let me take this further:* Walker *also holds lessons for those who write the past—suggesting how we who work in words might utilize humor, anachronism, absurdity, and the interpenetration of past and present to create a new kind history, one suitable for the sensibility of those who live in a media-saturated world (all of us!).*

The job of the historian . . . is not to reduplicate the
lost world of the past but to ask questions and answer
them.
                    —Louis Mink, *Historical Understanding*

Among academic historians there is a general, if
largely unarticulated, feeling that historical works
done on film, particularly dramatized history, can
never be as worthwhile or as "true" as historical works
done on the printed page. Such a notion seems to arise
from a sense that words are able to provide a serious
and complex past reality that film, with its supposed
need to entertain people, can never hope to match. To
show that such a view of the possibilities of history on
film is both shortsighted and wrong, I want to discuss
the ways in which a single historical film—*Walker*—
creates a past that is at once serious, complex, challenging, and "true" in its ability to render the meanings rather than the literal reality of past events. I also
want to show that a good part of the film's truth stems
from its unusual narrative strategies—strategies that
challenge the "realism" of both written history and the
standard dramatic or documentary historical film.
Strategies that expand the vocabulary in which history
can speak. Strategies that, were we interested in la-
bels, we might wish to name postmodern.

Directed by the British-born Alex Cox and released
by an American distributor, *Walker* (1987) plays with
and against many of the canons of both traditional
history and the standard historical drama.[1] As a work
of history, it successfully does the following three
things: (1) performs a variety of traditional historical

tasks; (2) goes beyond these tasks to create new ways of visualizing our relationship to the past, and (3) provides a "truth" that can stand beside all the written versions of William Walker's story that have appeared over the last 135 years. Like any good historical work, *Walker* recounts, explains, and interprets events in the past, and then attempts to justify the way it has undertaken these tasks. Like any work of history, the film situates itself within a tradition of historical questions, which means the answers provided by its story comment upon all the previous versions of the subject that have appeared. The film handles data and makes its argument within the format of a drama that utilizes five particular strategies: *Omission* and *Condensation* (both common to written history), *Alteration* and *Invention* (common to all works of history on film), and *Anachronism* (rare in any sort of history, except postmodern history).

The Story of Walker

Like any historical tale, that of William Walker may be told in a few words or in many. Both have been done. The longest work on Walker runs to 397 pages. Short, general histories of the pre–Civil War period dismiss him in a sentence or two. Let me provide here a mere outline of his life: Walker was a Nashville-born (1824) physician, attorney (New Orleans), and newspaperman (San Francisco) who, in what may be considered an extended gesture of Manifest Destiny, led a small band of adventurers into the state of Sonora, Mexico, in 1854 with the aim of creating a "free" country. Defeated by terrain, Mexican troops, and lack of support from home, Walker returned to the United States. A year later, he entered Nicaragua at the head of an army of 58 men—dubbed "the Immmortals" by the press—supposedly to help the Liberal Party in an ongoing civil war. By October 1855 he was commanding general of the Nicaraguan army; by July 1856, President of the Republic. During his time in office, Walker was an activist president who, among other things, instituted Negro slavery in Nicaragua and annulled the lucrative charter of Cornelius Vanderbilt's Accessory Transit Company, which controlled the chief route from the East Coast of the United States to California. Ten months later, after suffering severe military defeats at the hands of armies from all over Central America, and after being cut off from fresh recruits and military supplies from the United States, Walker torched the capital city of Granada, surrendered through the offices of a U.S. naval captain, and returned home, a hero to a goodly number of Americans. Twice more in the next three years he attempted to land in or near Nicaragua at the head of troops. In September 1860, he was captured and shot by the Honduran military. To his captors, he identified himself as "William Walker, President of Nicaragua."

Walker's story has been told and retold many times in both English and Spanish. The first account, written by his friend William V. Wells, appeared in 1856, even before Walker became president; the second, by Walker himself, was published four years later, just before his death. Since then, Walker's life and exploits have been the subject of at least six book-length historical works in the United States and several in Latin America; he has also been treated in chapters in several other works devoted either to U.S. diplomacy or to offbeat American adventurers and imperialists, and in a number of scholarly articles.[2]

To assess *Walker* the film it is important to underscore the following: virtually all the essential details that we know about Walker in Nicaragua today appear in the earliest accounts, including the books by Walker and Wells. Which is to say, all the studies of Walker utilize the same facts and recount essentially the same details concerning the who, how, where, and what that occurred when the Americans invaded Nicaragua. This is true for Walker's own actions and for the broader political-economic-social context in which he acted, the complicated economic and diplomatic maneuverings of both private interests and the governments of the United States, Great Britain, and various Central American countries. Yet if the details are clear, evaluations of the causes and the meanings of Walker's actions—for Walker, or for his supporters, or America, or the world—have shifted and changed over the decades. In short: for 140 years there has been no dispute over the facts of Walker's actions or the dimensions of his successes and his failures. The only real differences between historians surround such questions as: Why did he do what he did? What were his personal and political aims? Did his actions help or hurt the cause of America, or of "civilization"?

Stages of Interpretation

During his own time and throughout the late nineteenth century, books on William Walker in Nicaragua
generally took him on his own terms as an unqualified
hero, a stalwart patriot who was striving to spread the
benefits of American civilization to those who suffered
from Catholicism and bad government, a selfless man
who wished to regenerate Central America, a man
thwarted by short-sighted American politicians who
refused to extend economic aid or diplomatic recognition to his fledgling regime. This approach lasted into
the twentieth century. In 1913, E. Alexander Powell
included a chapter on Walker in *Gentlemen Rovers*, a
tribute to forgotten heroes, men who were important
in the expansion of the United States as they "stoutly
upheld American prestige and traditions in many far
corners of the world."[3]

Criticisms of Walker began in the same period, no
doubt reflecting the liberalizing attitudes toward
neighboring countries that were part of the Progressive era. The earliest work to fault him found problems less with the mission than with the man. In
Filibusters and Financiers (1916), William O. Scroggs
depicted a Walker whose shortcomings of character
and inability to understand human nature ruined a
good chance to help spread the benefits of American
civilization southward (newspapers and American
music are in particular singled out as "civilizing"
agents). The book depicted Walker's followers as heroes, fine pioneers who had developed the "supreme

civilization in California."[4] By misleading them, Walker destroyed a splendid opportunity to regenerate Central America.

In the 1930s, with dictatorships flexing their muscles all across Europe, writing on Walker took on a decidedly anti-fascist turn. William Green's *The Filibuster: The Career of William Walker* (1937), reeks with suspicion of Walker as a "ruthless dictator," a little man who aimed solely at power, and describes his men not as heroes but as a band of vagrants who came to fight, seduce, plunder, and kill.[5] These sentiments were not matched by any concern for the rights of Central Americans. Overtly contemptuous of all Latins, the author describes them in terms of traditional stereotypes—as a passionate, fickle, and treacherous people who love you one day and hate you the next.

More recent treatments of Walker provide an equally contemporary gloss on the man and his times. Albert Carr's *The World and William Walker* (1963) takes an approach that suits the decade in which it was written. At once anti-imperialist and psychoanalytic, the book portrays Walker as a harbinger of twentieth-century American relations with the world. The personal part of the volume focuses on Walker's sexuality, or lack of it, emphasizing his puritanical upbringing, his early interest in Walter Scott and the romantic tradition; indeed, the work suggests that sublimated sexuality accounts for the man's will to dominate, as well as for his career in Nicaragua. The public part of the book details the larger sphere in which Walker moved—the anti-slavery controversy that was to tear the United States apart; the detailed competition between American and British diplomats and military men. Here, Walker the ideologue of Manifest Destiny is portrayed as a semi-witting stalking horse for larger strategic and economic interests.

The most recent work on Walker, Frederic Rosengarten's *Freebooters Must Die* (1976), creates what one might call a multicultural interpretation. Making much of the fact that Walker is remembered in Central America as "a devil," the book claims that though he was interested in power it was not for power's sake alone. He was a man with a mission but a deeply flawed one. His mission to regenerate Central America would have instead created a slave empire, one that would have built and controlled a strategic canal from the Atlantic to the Pacific. If he had succeeded, Walker would have destroyed the precious Spanish-American cultural heritage and replaced with a ruthless Anglo-Saxon autocracy.

Despite these widely different interpretations, all the books provide a similar picture of the historical context in which Walker acted. All point to the Gold Rush, the Mexican American War, the increasing acrimony between North and South over the extension of slavery, and the acquisition of California as factors that helped fuel the expansionist mindset that took Walker (and other Americans) to Central America. All name that mindset Manifest Destiny and see it as not just a simple rationale for economic interests, but a peculiar national task, an odd sort of democratic imperialism, a sense that it was America's god-given mission to regenerate a benighted mankind. All detail the doings of Walker's economic counterpart, Cornelius Vanderbilt, whose mission is more simply understood—to promote and protect his monopoly over the lucrative sea-and-land route through Nicaragua.

The picture of Walker, the man—or at least of his personal characteristics and habits—is also remarkably consistent across the decades. All books agree that he was fearless, heroic, and financially incorruptible, a leader who was absolutely worshipped by his men. All show him as a stickler for discipline, a man who treated his own troops as harshly as natives over infractions. All portray Walker as a puritanical ascetic who did not drink or smoke, who ate moderately, and almost never laughed. (Concerning his sexual proclivities and activities, there are some sharp differences of interpretation. Some see Walker as asexual, some hint at possible homosexuality, and some suggest he had a discreet affair with a Nicaraguan woman of noble birth—and it is a great virtue of the film that it is able to suggest all three intepretations without insisting on any one of them. About Walker and sex one thing is clear: his sexual practices, whatever they were, disturbed contemporaries and have continued to disturb most historians, except for Carr, the only author to link sex and the drive for power.)

As with larger historical issues, the only disagreements over Walker the man come largely over the sorts of matters which an appeal to data cannot solve: Why did he develop from a democrat into a dictator? Where did he really stand on slavery? Why was he first so successful in Nicaragua and then why did he fail so miserably? Why did he burn down the capital city?

Walker and the Tasks of History

Anyone who has seen the film will already be familiar with many of the above details of William Walker's foray into Nicaragua. But the question of *Walker* as a piece of history—that is, of the film as a way of making the life and career of the man meaningful to us in the present—must be answered not merely by pointing to the existence of data but by assessing the way the data are utilized to create a historical world. My contention is that *Walker* takes the data familiar to all who have worked on the topic and, using a sense of historical awareness (shall we call it quasi-Marxist?) and aesthetic sensibility (postmodern) common to the late twentieth century, creates a William Walker suited to a contemporary historical consciousness. Certainly the mode of the film may be seen as a kind of black farce (closer at times to Monty Python than Eric Hobsbawm). But the film's humor and its blatant absurdities are crucial to its multidimensional portrait of Walker and his undertakings. Rather than detracting from the seriousness of the film, they are very much involved with the way the movie frames the past and fulfills four traditional tasks of any historical work—recounting, explaining, and interpreting the events of the past, and then justifying its fulfillment of those tasks.

Recounting. The William Walker whose story is re-
counted in the film is a figure whose complications
mirror larger issues in the American character, then
and now. He is portrayed as the emblem of Manifest
Destiny—self-centered (especially after the death of
his fiancée), single-minded, cold, fearless, ruthless,
and absolutely convinced of the righteousness of his
personal vision and actions. Unlike all written accounts, which seem unable to explain his increasingly
ruthless actions, the actor who plays Walker (Ed Harris) presents us with a character whose mystical and
sincere, if demagogic, democratic vision is corrupted
by the power (an eroticized power) he increasingly
acquires in Nicaragua. The broader context of the history is provided by scenes which depict the clash of
Walker's democratic imperialism with the overtly economic imperialism of Cornelius Vanderbilt, an imperialism whose ideology is static—as if capital is capital
and always acts in its own interest. Walker in the film
is, at least at the outset, an idealist—one whose ideals
lead to fanaticism. Vanderbilt is a cynic, whose ruth-
lessness leads to profit.

Explaining and Interpreting. The film shows both economic and democratic imperialism as born out of the
boundlessness of nineteenth-century America. It is the
land itself, one feels, that has created both Walker and
Vanderbilt. One image says it all: when the two men
meet face-to-face and one of the commodore's min-
ions speaks eloquently about the vast amounts of land
available "for the taking" in Nicaragua, the men are
sitting in a southwestern U.S. landscape virtually de-

void of humanity for as far as the eye can see. At that meeting, Walker overtly refuses to work with the unsavory Vanderbilt, but his own sense of mission lands him on the same side of the Nicaragua question. His form of imperialism, the film suggests, is older, more traditional than that of Vanderbilt. Clearly the film wants to show that capital utilizes the democratic missionary impulse as an ideology to cover whatever illegal or immoral actions it uses to make profits; it also depicts William Walker's personal corruption as of another sort—less economic than moral, an inevitable corrosion of the spirit when it is exposed to too much power, a corruption bound to wreak havoc and cause tragedy.

Justifying. Since motion pictures lack scholarly apparatus (footnotes, bibliography, appeal to authorities), this is always the most difficult historical task for a film to undertake. *Walker* makes its attempt in part by appealing to the historical Walker's real writings, used as voice-overs. This is, of course, a strategy pursued by many historical films. Much more important in *Walker* is the brilliant (postmodern) turn by which it uses a most unorthodox way of justifying its portrait—I refer to the film's overt appeal to the audience's knowledge (or sense) of how America has repeatedly intervened in Latin America (or elsewhere in the world—parallels to Viet Nam haunt the imagery of the film) and is clearly doing so in 1987, at the time the film is being made. The point is driven home by the many anachronisms which point directly to contemporary America. Walker's troops use Zippo lighters, drink Cokes, and smoke Marlboros. Walker appears on the covers of *Time* and *Newsweek*. Walker, in a parting statement to the Nicaraguans, insists: "We have a right to rule you. We will never leave you alone." The point about historical repetition and continuity is driven home by TV images beneath the final credits—President Reagan talking about Sandinistas; American troops on maneuvers in Honduras; dead and wounded Nicaraguan peasants who have been caught in attacks by Contra rebels.

Strategies of Representation

To create a Walker for our time, the film utilizes a number of strategies for rendering history: *Omission* and *Condensation, Alteration, Invention,* and *Anachronism.* The first two are integral to all forms of history, written, oral, or filmed; for no matter how detailed any portrait of the past, the data included are always only a highly selected and condensed sample of what could be included on a given topic. *Walker* tells us nothing of its subject's childhood, family, or schooling (save that he is a doctor and a lawyer); only hints at his medical and newspaper career in New Orleans and California; omits anything about the Mexican-American War, or the international diplomatic maneuverings between Great Britain, the United States, and Central American countries over regional issues; barely touches the slavery debate; and never specifies Walker's beliefs beyond the simplest level of exposition: "I hate slavery" or "I'm a social democrat" (a remark which also belongs under the category of *Anachronism*).

The strategies of *Alteration* and *Invention* are alike in that both depart from the norms of written history; indeed, both "create" historical fact (or incident) as a way of summarizing historical data that either cannot be expressed through visual images or whose expression in such images would be so inefficient that the (dramatic) structure of the work would be impaired. The two differ in that *Alteration* changes documentable historical fact by restructuring incidents or events (altering time, place, participants), while *Invention* freely creates characters and incidents. (Note: What I refer to here are major sorts of inventions, for as I have argued elsewhere, the most "accurate" works of dramatic history on film will always contains huge doses of what we might call small invention, acts of creation which historians who work in words will call fiction. Because the camera demands more specificity than historians can ever know, all historical settings are what might be called proximate fictions. Similarly, costume, dialogue, gesture, action, the very use of dramatic structure—all these are full of small fictions used, at best, to create larger historical "truths," truths which can be judged only by examining the extent to which they engage the arguments and "truths" of our existing historical knowledge on any given topic.)

All of the major *Alterations* in *Walker* can be seen and justified as ways of expressing metaphoric or symbolic historical truths. For example: By opening the film with a battle in Mexico and misplacing (or re-placing) his fiancée's death after that battle, the film makes us focus immediately on the relationship between Manifest Destiny and violence that is its very historical core, and portrays Walker (as do written works) as a man once torn between the personal and the political until her death turned him into a wholly public man. By having Walker march forward on foot dressed in a (historically documented) black suit during horrendously violent battles rather than riding a horse (as he did), the film provides an indelible image of the man's fearlessness and unshrinking determination described in all contemporary accounts. By collapsing two Nicaraguan political figures into a single leader, whom Walker first sets up as a puppet president and later executes, the film underscores the irrelevance of actual Nicaraguans to Walker's ventures and policies. The same point is made when Walker has trouble remembering the names of the Nicaraguan leaders or when his soldiers complain that there seems to be no difference between Liberal Nicaraguans, for whom they fight, and Conservatives, their enemies. (Again, Viet Nam and other recent interventions abroad are clearly implied.)

The *Inventions* of the film also work as apposite, symbolic historical assertions. For example: By making Walker's chief lieutenant a black American (the historical record shows no such individual, though some blacks did serve with Walker), the film points to his original antislavery beliefs and shows that his later introduction of slavery into Nicaragua was neither easy nor foreordained, but rather the result of the perceived necessity to obtain both a labor pool and the support of Southern American states. By showing his affair with the aristocratic Dona Yrena, the film suggests how easily the democratic Walker climbed into bed with Nicaragua's upper classes. Her subsequent attack on him with a pistol becomes an apt rendering of how quickly and violently this unnatural alliance fell apart. (Through the skilled acting of Ed Harris, the film is able to suggest multiple interpretations of Walker's sexuality; the affair with Dona Yrena shows him as sexually inexperienced; scenes with the soldier named Timothy not so subtly suggest homoerotic attachments; still other scenes suggest masochism, or the sublimation of sexuality into the quest for power. In such visual hints, which work to suggest that multiple interpretations may all be true, the film achieves a sort of simultaneous interpretive complexity that would be less likely in a written text; certainly no historian to date has suggested that Walker might be multisexual.)

No doubt the most important of the inventions is the meeting between Walker and Vanderbilt. Historically, the two men never met face-to-face, yet their angry encounter in an obviously mythic space—alongside a railroad track in Arizona, decades before trains came to the West—is crucial to the meaning of the film. In this clash between powerful individuals, the two sorts of American imperialisms—economic and democratic—stake out the terms of their debate with each other and with the larger world. Their exchange reveals the clash of greed and self-interest, the fervent if misplaced idealism, and the hidden complicities which have fueled American expansionism for a hundred and fifty years. To portray this same conflict, the historian who works in words would have created this encounter on the page, by outlining the ideology or mindset of each man. That ideas compete in neat paragraphs on a page is no less a fiction than the onscreen meeting between Walker and Vanderbilt. The difference is that this sort of written fiction has become an unquestioned convention of history. Needing an image, film works in a different way. Yet each technique of rendering this quarrel merely utilizes a particular medium in a suitable way to talk about the past.

To make this assertion is to run against the common but mistaken notion that the historical film somehow provides an accurate window onto the world of the past. Elsewhere I have argued that film cannot ever do this, for it is always a construction that points to the world of the past by providing proximate images of vanished realities. *Walker* makes certain that it cannot possibly be taken for a window onto history by the overt and creative strategy of *Anachronism*. The Zippo lighters, Coke bottles, and Marlboros used by Walker's troops, the *Time* and *Newsweek* magazines with his picture on the cover, the hip contemporary language, the glimpse of a Mercedes roaring by a carriage, the computer terminals in Vanderbilt's office, and the final evacuation of the Americans from Granada in helicopters—all these images point to the inevitable interpenetration of past and present. Beyond destroying the surface realism of the film, they work to demystify the pretensions of professional history, cast into doubt notions of historical distance and objectivity, and insist that the questions we take to the past always arise from our current concerns; that, in fact, it is impossible for us to see the world of Walker, or any historical realm, without images of automobiles, helicopters, and computer terminals in our minds.

Walker's use of *Alteration* and *Invention* is shared—less consciously, to be sure—by all historical films. *Anachronism* is also not an original device, but no other historical film has ever used it so overtly and continuously in an effort to keep us aware of the continuity of historical questions and issues. Another important part of the film's creative strategy for rendering the past comes in its use of the soundtrack in an effort to render historical complexities not easily obtainable by the written word. *Walker* opens with upbeat Latin music that is wholly at odds with the images of violent death and destruction during a battle in Sonora, Mexico. For the rest of the film, sound continues to play against image to provide a double vision of historical reality. Or is it a multiple vision? Joyous music at odds with destruction provides not only a critique of war itself, but also of a long tradition of historical films which utilize music to make battle glamorous and heroic. Another contradiction between sound and image comes in the voice-over narration, taken in part from Walker's memoirs. Here the leader's lofty, idealized descriptions of the expeditionary force are repeatedly undercut by actions onscreen. The voice speaks of cultural reforms and we see natives being flogged; it speaks of regenerating a nation and we see American soldiers drinking, fighting, stealing from natives, and assaulting females of more than one species. ("The colonel says it's a democracy," shouts one soldier, as he climbs into a sheep pen and lowers his pants.)

The doubled vision presented by playing sound against image and the humor involved in odd juxtapositions seem to work in a variety of ways. Distanced from Walker and his men, we can study their behavior without the normal tugs of sentiment or patriotism. The doubling also hints at the perennial gap between history and behavior, official rhetoric and experience, the language utilized by the distant observer and the scholar and the realities it purports to encompass. By highlighting such contradictions, *Walker* directs us to the problems of all historical representation and understanding. Quite consciously, the film delivers a story at once invented, (perhaps) postmodern, and, I would argue, true—a story that comments on our past and present and never lets us forget that the two always interpenetrate.

In breaking with the normal conventions of the historical motion picture, *Walker* highlights the limits of Hollywood's favorite way of constructing a world on the screen—illusionist realism. Working against the far edges of the historical genre, its sometimes farcical, layered history suggests a complexity to historical knowledge that a traditional single-line narrative could never handle. The film's argument is certainly clear enough: intervention abroad based upon Manifest Destiny—democratic or economic, past or present—is bound to corrupt and wreak havoc on both Americans and those they wish to help or exploit. Yet for all the single-minded strength of this moral stance, the overtly innovative strategies and black humor of the film point toward the contested nature of historical knowledge.

To put it simply: From the opening moments, *Walker* outrageously problematizes its own assertions—and also teaches you how to "read" the history you are about to see. It begins with a battle scene in which ragtag Mexican soldiers run across a field to the sound of upbeat Latin music. The screen goes black and then we see in bold red letters "This is a True Story," followed by images of American troopers exploding out of a farmhouse in a kind of slowmotion death ballet while the joyous music continues. Here at the outset of the film we are shown that whatever the "truth" of the story, it is not a literal truth. The screen cannot be a window onto the past—not just because the window has been blown away but because we know that in the real world men do not die in slow motion to the sound of dance music. *Walker* warns us at the outset that the historical truths it delivers are not to be taken as reality, and suggests that the literal reconstruction of the past is not at stake in this—or in any other project of historical understanding. What should matter, the film suggests, is the seriousness which which we ask and answer, in whatever form of address or medium, questions about the meaning of the past.

· 7 ·

Sans Soleil

The Documentary as (Visionary) Truth

The following essay was originally delivered as an oral commentary on Chris Marker's Sans Soleil, *after a screening at the Neighborhood Film and TV Project, located at International House in Philadelphia. One of the glorious accomplishments of nonfiction cinema,* Sans Soleil *is known as a filmmaker's film, a dense work that can be baffling to those who expect cinema to deliver a linear, straightforward, clearly defined story or argument. At once a political thinker and a poet, Marker is obsessed with the meaning of time and the power of the past to shape our lives—which is to say he is a kind of historian, a historian who knows there can be no real separation between the personal, the political, and the historical. Because my words assume an audience still full of the images of* Sans Soleil, *this essay may present some difficulties for those who have not seen the film. Yet to summarize it is impossible. I can do no better than to describe the film as a free-form visual essay in which an unknown woman reads and comments upon letters she receives from a friend—a free-lance cameraman who has been traveling around the globe for decades and has become interested in those extreme poles of survival, Africa and Japan. We see images of political struggle and social life, of work and religious ritual, all of which have been, presumably, shot by this same cameraman,*

*who continually wonders aloud about the process of representing
the world in images, of creating memories on film, while a Japanese friend of his, Hayao, breaks up the images of memory the
filmmaker has created by distorting them on a sophisticated syn-
thesizer. For anyone who has not seen* Sans Soleil, *this synopsis
may not be much to go on, yet I think that my essay will convey,
even to those unfamiliar with the work, something of the film's
thrust and complexity. This is due, in part, to the fact that I deal
largely with the text of the work (in truth, that is all I could do, for
the images of the film are so rich, varied, swift, and dense that there
would be no way to convey a sense of them in words). It is due in
part, too, to the mode of writing—my language is meant to evoke
feeling and meaning rather than to analyze the work's accomplishments. At the very least, those who have not seen* Sans Soleil *will
get some sense of the surprising variety of historical and philosophi-
cal questions which a nonfiction film can raise—at least in the mind
of one historian.*

Sans Soleil is a dazzling and difficult film. Dazzling and
difficult for anyone who views it, including film critics
and theoreticians. I have now seen it six times and
cannot pretend to grasp it fully, though each viewing
gives me a better feeling for its themes and obsessions.
As with any work of art, there can be no single key to
what *Sans Soleil* means because it overflows with more
meanings than we would ever have time to fathom or
record.

The form of the film has been described in many
ways. One critic, calling it a "no-man's-land of documentary images and oblique fiction," claims it "has no
subject except the consciousness, the memory of the
man who shot it." Another has termed it an editor's

film, one which expands the possibilities of the medium in its mixture of fictional and documentary elements. Others have said it is a work which does not answer questions but generates them. A work which shows that "high seriousness can be entertaining." A film that "resists categories" in a strange blend of elements from the ethnographic film and the French "nouveau roman." The aim of the film has been seen in different ways—to "recover what is lost," to find the "secret structure" of things, to discredit "any unitary narrative of history."[1]

To call it multitextured and layered, to claim it is a film with incredibly rich imagery and narration, is to indulge in serious understatement. My aim here is to reflect upon the meanings of *Sans Soleil*, but I must confess that there is no way of doing justice to its complexities in a short essay—or even in a long one. What I will do is read it in a way that nobody, to the best of my knowledge, has yet attempted—as a work of history. Offbeat history: certainly. Postmodern history: without doubt. But perhaps a far better term for it is visionary history, a phrase that not only includes more than one meaning but comes closer to expressing the intense experience of image, language, and sound that the film provides.

In looking at *Sans Soleil* as a work of history, I shall dwell primarily on the meaning conveyed by the spoken text. My justification for doing so is not just that the intense, poetic narration in the film is as provocative and productive of meanings as the images we see, but also that words always link together the images and carry the arguments of all nonfiction films. This point was made by Chris Marker himself in a 1958 documentary entitled *Letter from Siberia*. This film consists of three different sets of narration spoken over a repeated, identical series of images of farming in Siberia, commentaries that reflect three different world views: communist, socialist, and capitalist. The director's aim was to demonstrate "how sounds transform images, how ideologies manipulate cognition, how three separate narratives can be lifted from one visual context."[2]

My historical reading begins with a quotation from one of the many letters written to the narrator of *Sans Soleil* by, ostensibly, the director of the film: "I am writing you all this from another world, a world of appearances. In a way, the two worlds communicate with each other. Memory is to one what History is to the other. An impossibility. Legends are born out of the need to decipher the indecipherable. Memories must make do with their delirium, with their drift. A moment stopped would burn like a frame of film blocked before the furnace of the projector."[3]

Here is an entry into *Sans Soleil* as history, a special kind of history, a history that parallels memory in its need to make sense out of the senseless. Both history and memory in this world (these worlds) must mean not (just) publicly, but personally (the level on which history must always, eventually, mean). This is a film not only about the meaning of memory and history, but about their very possibility in an age where media have become our way of dealing not just with reality, but with those vanished moments we call the past. It is a film about what the narrator, or the filmmaker, can rescue from time; what images he can capture to provide enough meaning to allow us to live. And this even while knowing the limitation of these images, the ones he and we record and the ones he and we create.

In form the film is an essay, a series of simultaneous verbal and visual reflections. Let's call it a new form of history for a visual age: a history which does not consist of assembling data into some kind of logical argument, but in ruminating over the possibilities of memory and history, personal experience and public events—and the relationships among them. And how we might use these things, or our images of them, to understand ourselves and our world.

These reflections are not those of everyone, but of a very specific filmmaker with a specific set of memories and experiences—one who has been around the world many times, who has shot ethnographic films, leftist films, revolutionary films, guerrilla films in Africa, Iceland, Russia, Europe, America, and Japan. A man whose comings and goings have been, in his words, not a search for contrasts but part of a journey "to the two extreme poles of survival"—in the case of this film, to Guinea-Bissau and Japan. Both are non-Western countries, but there are vast differences between them. One is an impoverished, Third World realm, and the other a high-tech, economic superpower. His travels have not made the filmmaker jaded, but no longer is he searching for the heroic, the romantic, the unusual: "Now, only banality still interests me." In *Sans Soleil* he stalks it "with the relentlessness of a bounty hunter."

So we have a character searching for something—but what? Memory itself? Perhaps. He claims to have spent his life "trying to understand the function of remembering." Clearly he does remember, perhaps too many things. But the only way he can remember is by relying on the visual media, whose trickiness and ambiguity can never be forgotten, least of all by one who manipulates them so well: "I wonder how people remember things who don't film, don't photograph, don't tape." As if to underline the point, elsewhere he ruminates: "I remember the month of January in To-kyo—or I remember the images I filmed of the month of January. They have substituted themselves for my memory. They *are* my memory." But this does not answer the obsessive question: What is the function of remembering?

The filmmaker uses the media to remember and yet he is highly skeptical of media images. This is the point of "the machine," a sophisticated electronic synthe-sizer that can manipulate and alter moving images. Named the Zone (in homage to a film by the Soviet director Andrei Tarkovsky), the machine is utilized by the filmmaker's friend, Hayao, who says: "If the im-ages of the present don't change, then change the images of the past." But what kind of history is this—is it not the history we in a media culture live? What happens to that present, to those images, as they be-come past? They are emptied of content and turned

into sheer visual beauty. Hayao can do this with anything: riots, war, destruction, even death can be rendered harmless and lovely by the machine. And indeed, by the end of the film, its own images have
entered Hayao's Zone, and we watch their meaning
being beautified and changed. So how can one remember a world, or have a history, when the images
on which our sense of the past is based can be
changed, altered, even bled of meaning?

The problematics of representing "reality" or remembering the past do not keep us from the need to
do so. In memory, in history, and in images, it seems,
lies our humanity, our connection to our world and
each other. At least this is the area in which Marker
constructs his film—or rather Sándor Krasna does. For
it is letters written by this fictional character named
Krasna which are read by the female narrator. And it
is his words which are spoken by her ("He told me"
and "He wrote me") except for those occasions when
the words seem to be her own, those moments when
she speaks directly.

This uncertainty of address is part of the deep tex-
turing of the filmic world, whose verbal and visual
narrative levels are extremely complex. Sometimes we
don't know who is addressing us. At other times, the
relationship between the images and the narration is
problematic. Sometimes the words seem to explain or
relate to the images; sometimes not. Even the time
frame in which all these things are viewed, written,
spoken, and constructed is uncertain. Many of the
images were shot in Japan sometime between 1979

and 1981. Others were shot in various parts of the world—France, Holland, Iceland, Guinea-Bissau, the Cape Verde Islands, San Francisco—across three decades. As in the unconscious, all images are equally present in the world of this film.

"His" world—that of Marker or Krasna—begins with an image that he calls "Happiness": three smiling children on a road in Iceland. They are abruptly replaced by an image of armed military aircraft, rising up an elevator to the deck of a carrier. The message seems clear. The world of the film lies after the fall. Later this becomes explicit in the Josenkai section, shot in a museum which consists of displays of pairs of stuffed animals fornicating. If "one would like to believe in a world before the fall," even after the fall, we must go on.

His world has two poles, with contrasting conceptions of time: the West and the non-West, clock time and traditional time. And certainly more than one kind of the latter. He tells us that the great question of the nineteenth century concerned the divisions of space and that of the twentieth concerns the "coexistence of different concepts of time." He shows us different kinds of time in Japan and Africa. Japan itself seems simultaneously modern and traditional, a realm of clock time and seasonal time, of regulated time and timelessness. His interest is largely in the latter category. Not in the economic miracle (though he pays homage to it), but in local festivals; in the many "villages" of Tokyo, the tiny neighborhoods into which the megalopolis breaks down at night; in local shrines and graveyards; above all, in the solemn graveyard for cats.

One thing which connects cultures in Africa and Japan—and distinguishes them from those of the West—is the presence of animism, the importance of animals to humans. They serve as mediating figures between us and a world of gods. They are innocently sexual (though we put them to semi-pornographic, semi-divine uses). They are examples of virtue (the loyalty of the dog Hachiko, who died waiting for his vanished owner and whose stone statue at Shibuya station is now a place of worship), of beauty (the emus that still exist on the Île-de-France). They are in touch with the traditional cycles of time. They are part of our link to nature, to death. In Japan the same flowers are used at funerals of animals and humans. In Japan, people mourn the deaths of giant pandas more than the deaths of prime ministers. It is a country whose practices stand as a critique of those of the West, for they suggest we have lost touch with something important. Somebody tells him: "The partition that separates life and death does not appear as thick to us as it does to a Westerner."

What of the human historical world? Talking of the Heian Age (Japan's classic age, the tenth to twelfth centuries) while following a rocket launching into orbit, the filmmaker tells us that that period was an example of how the "complicated strategies of rulers" can be less important to a culture than a "small group of idlers"—people like the aristocratic court lady Sei Shōnagon, who spent her time indulging in love affairs, writing melancholy poetry, and making lists of beautiful things that "quicken the heart." She ignored the problems of the larger world, and yet for centuries Shōnagon has been far better remembered than all the thundering politicians and emperors of her age.

What of revolution, that modern dream of transformation? The one in Guinea-Bissau, which overthrew the government of Portugal, almost made the filmmaker believe in the possibility of a new revolution in Europe. But it failed, and nobody remembers it now: "History throws its empty bottles out of the window." "History only tastes bitter to those who expected it to be sugar-coated." And what if revolution were to succeed? Then the real work begins and it is boring, unromantic work.

Once a believer, the filmmaker seems to have given up on revolution. Not in the spirit of revolution; not in the need for it in certain parts of the world. But he has seen too much, filmed too much, and learned too much to work for it—or perhaps to work for anything (other than salvation?) accomplished in that time known as history. Only those, he says, who have "amnesia of the future," those who are blessedly free of knowing what is to come, the way human enterprises always decline or grow corrupt (like the revolution in Guinea-Bissau), can act blissfully in history. Amnesia shields them from the judgment of history: "She doesn't care, she understands nothing, she has only one friend—horror, that has a name and face."

Revolutions fail or succeed and the revolutionaries kill each other off. Yet despite such failures or successes, one can still hope. For the filmmaker, hope remains alive in the great battles being undertaken by students and farmers as they try to prevent the construction of Narita airport. It's like the sixties all over again. Exasperating as that generation could be, he loved it because its members exemplified something Che Guevara put into words when he said he "trembled with indignation every time an injustice is committed in the world." But today's kids are different. It is not clear that they know the "secret": that life is not something you can seek but something you are. That they, in fact, are life and will, before they know it, be eaten like donuts. This is equally true of the colorful rebels, the Takenoko, and the proper young ladies who, on officially becoming adults at twenty, on Adults' Day, are given free long-distance calls to their homes as a present by the phone company: "How long will it be until they all forget the secret?" "Pacman" is the real metaphor for today's life: no matter how many victories one scores at the game, it "always comes a cropper in the end."

And yet, however confined by history, the film seems to suggest that one can somehow be happy in this realm of time we call history. That surely is the lesson of the kamikaze pilot who writes a farewell note before he dives to destruction. He may not favor the war he fights, but his message is clear: that Japan must "live free in order to live eternally." He knows that he is going to his death as if he were a machine, and yet he has done what is right and can say "In my heart I am happy."

What about Japan today? How is life in this electronic megalopolis? There is something human in its rhythms and its collective dreams, however tawdry— even the dreams of subway passengers of both sexes, lusting after sex or violence or some combination of the two that exists on a human scale. Japan's festivals are suffused with a sense of the past—full of an ability to keep in touch with the other world through reverence for gods, animals, spirits of inanimate objects like dolls and debris. Such objects too can have their moments of transcendence. There is something to be learned here about the West, about its "unbearable vanity which has never ceased to privilege being over non-being, what is spoken over what is left unsaid."

Is happiness possible, the film seems to ask—happiness in this realm of time? Once again we see the image of the three children in Iceland. Then the filmmaker tells us a story of the visitor from the future, from 4001, who has lost the ability to forget, who is burdened with total recall, with "memory anesthetized." It is all too much. Somehow, we need our memories to be selective and imperfect. The visitor's desire is to understand something in the past, something that exists in our day but has been forgotten in the future: unhappiness. But he cannot understand it, any more than people from rich countries can understand people from poor ones. He can only get a vague intimation of unhappiness in the songs of a cycle by Moussorgsky, a cycle entitled "Sans Soleil"— only music can express the sad dimensions of our condition.

What happens to happiness, to history itself, when everything disappears, buried in lava in a volcanic eruption, such as that in Iceland which destroyed the world of those three happy children? Wiped everything away, save for those images on film. Now that moment exists only in memory, for us and for the filmmaker, who must go on pointing his camera at the world and making sense of it in images and sound. Happiness for him and for us does not seem to be a collective dream, as it is for the Japanese, but something individual. He can make obeisance to all the offbeat spirits and gods of Tokyo—those of broken cars, torn-up and unmailed letters. But his world is that of Hayao's Zone, where every image, every meaning can become something else. He likes that shifting, malleable world because "it speaks to the part of us which insists on drawing profiles on prison walls. A piece of chalk to follow the contours of what is not, or is no longer, or is not yet. The handwriting each one of us will use to compose his own list of things that 'quicken the heart' . . . In that moment poetry will be made by everyone, and there will be emus in the Zone."

Will there be another letter from Sándor Krasna? From the filmmaker? The film ends with this question—suggesting that if there is to be more, we must be the ones to write the words and create the images.

That *Sans Soleil* is obsessed and suffused with memory, anyone who sees it has to agree. But is it a work of history? That may be harder to accept. Certainly not history as we know it in its written forms—not even history as it usually appears on the screen. But I see it as a possible form of history, one that is densely visual and verbal, that privileges neither the word nor the image but somehow sets them against each other to achieve new sorts of understanding. A history that includes many voices, or one voice in many guises, allowing for the speaking of more than one kind of truth, of even contradictory truths. A history that renders a kind of knowledge that we do not exactly know how to judge in normal historical terms, for it lies outside all known genres and kinds of historical discourse. Certainly this is a kind of history that has escaped the ghost of positivism that lingers in the machine of the social sciences—escaped any idea that history consists of data arranged into neat building blocks, each one a part of a grand edifice of knowledge.

Ultimately the center of this film is Hayao's Zone. One critic has described this as a region where hierarchy no longer holds sway, where there exists "a new kind of objectivity, a new way of understanding representations and of constructing them as a challenge to the ossified fables of history." If this is true of the Zone, it is also true of the film that frames the Zone. Like Hayao, the filmmaker suggests that we—like him—must learn to create our own histories. That public history is no more than a collective dream—and sometimes a highly destructive one. A dream lost in the vortex of some ultimate mystery—perhaps even a dream of some god. For our politics, our poems, our children, our favorite places, our lives, our deaths can be shifted into new shapes, colors, and meanings depending upon who sits at the board of control. We all have access to some such boards of control, those of our own minds and memories. Only when we create our own histories can we create those individual meanings by which we acquire the faith to go on living in this realm where pain, passion, despair, hope, and love ultimately remain as images, bits of knowledge, abstractions that others may manipulate at their own boards, knowledge that may have little to do with what we ever felt, or thought, or hoped, or knew, or understood. History is a realm where we know we can never outlast the changes that will come to it and us, singly and together, and yet where we must live and film and remember each day as if we can.

III

THE FUTURE OF THE PAST

▾ ▾ ▾

· 8 ·

Re-visioning History

Contemporary Filmmakers and the
Construction of the Past

*Early on in my research on the historical film, I became deeply
interested in how filmmakers from different cultural traditions
represent the past in ways that could make the mainstream Hollywood film (at least to me) seem visually, dramatically, and intellectually dull. When I was asked to review one of the following books,
I took the opportunity to add several others and use them as a point
of departure for exploring the historical film in three traditions
obsessed by the past and determined, so it seems, to render its
meanings in new ways: Africa, Latin America, and Germany.
Typically, not one of the authors of the nine volumes deigns to
consider the history film as a separate category. This blindness to
the way film reconfigures our notions of the past is yet another
reason we historians need to explore the realm of film—particularly
the past as rendered in lands where its meaning can seem immediately crucial to personal and cultural identity.*

Brazilian Cinema, edited by Randal Johnson and Robert
Stam (Austin: University of Texas, 1988)

Cinema and Social Change in Latin America: Conversations with Filmmakers, edited by Julianne Burton (Austin: University of Texas, 1986)

The Cinema of Ousmane Sembene: A Pioneer of African Film, by Françoise Pfaff (Westport, Conn.: Greenwood, 1984)

The Cuban Image; Cinema and Cultural Politics in Cuba, by Michael Chahan (Bloomington: Indiana University, 1985)

From Hitler to Heimat: The Return of History as Film, by Anton Kaes (Cambridge: Harvard University, 1989)

New German Film: The Displaced Image, by Timothy Corrigan (Austin: University of Texas, 1983)

Third World Film Making and the West, by Roy Armes (Berkeley: University of California, 1987)

Tradition Orale et Nouveaux Medias, edited by Victor Bachy (Brussels: OCIC, 1989)

Twenty-Five Black African Filmmakers: A Critical Study, with Filmography and Bio-Bibliography, by Françoise Pfaff (Westport, Conn.: Greenwood, 1988)

The setting: a classroom in a village hut in Senegal. On the wall, maps of Africa and France. Barefoot young students, crowded together at long tables, repeat by rote phrases that their teacher reads from a book. Phrases that praise the accomplishments "of our ancestors, the fair-haired Gauls."

Call it the primal scene. The classroom is at once real and symbolic; the filmed moment self-referential; the purpose educational. Remember that everywhere in the Third World the motion picture screen has always been filled with the faces of Americans and Europeans whose personal problems, stemming from ambition and love, speak of a rich world that can be no more than a fantasy to the audience. Just as bad—no, worse—are the films with Third World settings, films in which the natives are not masterful like the whites, but docile servants, vicious enemies, buffoons. ("We always cheered for Tarzan," says an African filmmaker.) Either sort of image helps to rob a people of their heritage, their culture, their very identity. What to do? Fight the image with the image. Recreate your own world on the motion picture screen.

Call it the primal scene for this essay as well. The black faces of the children in contrast with the words they speak provide a uniquely filmic moment of meaning. It is a historical moment, too, one that points directly toward the theme of this article: How can motion pictures re-vision history? Not that all the books considered here specifically take up this topic, or even deal directly with the historical film. But all are deeply concerned with how film can be used to come to grips with the legacy of the past. Together they show how in the last quarter-century filmmakers in Africa, Latin America, and Germany have dealt with history on the screen in a variety of unusual and innovative ways. My aim in bringing them together is to explore these innovations, to understand the varied ways in which motion pictures can be used to speak about the past; to situate historians in relation to film and history, and film and history in relation to each other.

Practically and theoretically, interactions between the discipline of history and the practices of the visual media are problematic. Consider the scene above: clearly it is historical, but how can the historian relate to it? The scene is undated, the village unspecified. No doubt a similar scene occurred thousands of times over tens of decades in hundreds of locations in French colonies. No doubt it occurred many times in the village of the director Safi Faye, who has put it on the screen at the beginning of *Fad'jal*, a work that—among other things—goes on to visualize the oral history of her village. Yet questions hover in the wake of the scene. About, say, its specificity: Is that really a classroom or a set? Are the children really students or are they actors? More important: How would different answers reflect on the issue of historical truth?

By themselves, these questions may seem inconsequential. But they point to larger issues involved in any discussion of the possibility of doing history on film. It is not an easy subject to talk about sensibly. Something like media hype seems to rub off on sober professors. Astonishing claims are made for and against motion pictures. Partisans would have you believe that only film, with its world of moving images, can hope to approximate the complexity of historical experience. Opponents see history on film as a travesty that inevitably must fictionalize, romanticize, and oversimplify the past. Even academics who study the media hardly take the possibility of doing history on film seriously. Looking through the world on the screen, they treat the historical film not as a way of thinking about the past but as a reflection of the values of the period in which it was made.

These reactions are based on the sort of film made in Hollywood (or its suburbs in London, Paris, Calcutta, Tokyo). We all know this film too well; its aim is clearly not enlightenment, but entertainment; not truth, but profit. But the Hollywood model is not the only kind of history on film. Not at all. In the twenties, Soviet filmmakers created new visions of the past (e.g., *Potemkin* and *Oktober*) that we still admire, if more as art than as history. More recently, filmmakers from around the globe have been taking up the challenge of dealing seriously with the past. Their works are part of a larger historical moment, the arrival of a non-commercial cinema anxious to recapture particular traditions from decades—even centuries—of (mis)representation by outsiders. To fully understand their innovations, one needs to experience their films. Yet here we must be content with words—which is to say, with both their limitations and their strengths. Only words can ask the questions that guide this inquiry: To what extent can historians accept history on film as valid? How can we judge such history? What are the implications—or challenges—of the historical film for written history?

> Whenever you make a historical film, whether it is set two decades or two centuries in the past, you are referring to the present.
> —Humberto Solas

Let's begin with the "struggle" (that favorite leftist word) against Hollywood. A struggle—as Roy Armes shows in his superb work, *Third World Film Making and the West*—against the two faces of Hollywood: the Hollywood that, through various economic policies and political strategems, has dominated film markets throughout the world, and the Hollywood that creates the particular kind of motion picture which we often take to be the *only* kind of motion picture. This dramatic film—a self-mystifying vehicle of Western beliefs—always focuses on the emotional life of the individual hero, the man or woman (almost always the man) whose desires for love, success, power, happiness, or even a better world take precedent over any social or political goals. Such men and women exist in a "realistic" world that is carefully constructed through a variety of techniques (matched sight-lines of characters, shots and reverse shots, seamless editing) whose chief aim is to hide themselves. The result is a work that seems not at all constructed. We stare through the window of the screen directly at a "real" world.

Not all Third World filmmakers refuse to make such films or object to turning a nice profit, and a major virtue of Armes's book is its recognition of the complexity of response to Western film. In Bombay, Cairo, Rio de Janeiro, Mexico City, Manila, and other major media centers, Hollywood-type industries have grown and flourished. Yet like Hollywood, this commercial Third World cinema has been challenged by a cinema of opposition. In the sixties the challenge began with the so-called "Third Cinema." Marxist in orientation, this movement aimed to "decolonize" both the industry and the image, to replace screen fantasy with "throbbing, living reality."[1] No surprise that Third Cinema was the creation of artists and intellectuals who were themselves highly Westernized. No surprise either that it suffered from a central paradox: aspiring to be of the people, Third Cinema produced films that were rarely popular.[2]

For history on film, popularity is less the issue than vision. Here the Third Cinema may be judged a success. Oppositional filmmakers did create new filmic strategies, new ways of thinking on the screen about social, political, and cultural issues. Yet while many of their works dealing with history are mentioned by Armes, his book does not recognize the historical film as a category. How to explain this? One might argue that "history" itself is a Western project. But evidence exists for a simpler explanation: filmmakers have simply been too caught up in national liberation struggles to explore history systematically. They have set films in the past for the same reason they have set them in the present, have used history as a way of commenting upon current problems of race, class, gender, ethnicity, and nationalism. Ahistorical? Presentist? Perhaps. But not a wholly unfamiliar strategy to academics. Not so different from the reasons for the rise of such recent fields as ethnic, feminist, and gay history.

> Black African films . . . are instruments which allow us to affirm our identity, to fight cultural imperialism as well as economic and political oppression.
>
> —Gaston Kabore

Nowhere has the desire to recover control of one's images been stronger than in Africa. Anyone who has encountered even a few African films will know something of this already. Anyone who has not can follow this theme (with some difficulty) in the pages of Françoise Pfaff's compendious *Twenty-Five Black African Filmmakers*. More a work of reference than criticism, the book makes no systematic argument as it chronicles the diversity of sub-Saharan film in the quarter-century since its origins. The representative 25 (out of more than 250 living) filmmakers are dealt with in individual chapters. Only in the brief preface are their common themes even mentioned: to reject "alien stereotypes in favor of realistic images of Africa" and to depict "African realities . . . as a tool for progress through self-examination and self-actualization."[3]

Such tasks call for representing a heritage that colonialism ignored and repressed. But this does not imply seeing history in Western terms. Though her work describes films set in the past, Pfaff—like Armes—does not recognize the historical film as a category. In this she follows her subjects. Of the two most common sorts of Western history film—those based upon actual people or events, and those in which the characters may be fictional but certain historical moments or movements are intrinsic to the development of the plot and action—Africa has almost none of the first and only a few of the second. These few, set in the recent past, relate the problems of post-independence: social dislocations due to development, student unrest, political and moral corruption, and the lingering hold of former colonial masters on the new native leadership. Shall we say they constitute a kind of "instant history," one whose Hollywood forms may well reflect that postcolonial countries now live with a Western sense of time?

In dealing with more remote periods, Africans depart from Hollywood conventions to create films that seem consonant with an oral tradition. Common are tales of village or tribal ancestors and heroes, tales that aim less to recreate the look or the political issues of the past than to reconstitute its enduring lessons. Often the ethnographic and the historical collapse together. The repetitive motions of women hoeing in a field, the ceremonies and dances that honor the gods, the actions of an individual king or warrior or thief—all exist in a world where chronology is less important than morality. Missing here are a linear sense of time, a desire to analyze cause and effect, a need to provide naturalistic explanations for how and why things occur.

African history comes to us not through the image alone, but also through the words of a *griot,* one of those traditional storytellers responsible for tribal memory. Today such figures are increasingly marginal to African life, and more than one film charts their decline in the modern world (*Sa Dagga,* 1982, by Momar Thiam of Senegal, for example). This loss provides an opportunity to make a special claim for motion pictures: that what the *griot* was to tribal Africa, the filmmaker is to Africa today. Hinted at in Pfaff, this argument is central to several articles in *Tradition Orale et Nouveaux Medias*, a group of essays from a colloquium held at the Tenth Pan-African Film Festival in 1987. What, you wonder, do filmmaker and *griot* have in common? Both have the task of linking the worlds of past and present; both tell stories to ensure cultural continuity and survival. Yet the differences are clear as well. As an oral performer, the *griot* alters his story in response to the audience reaction; for the filmmaker, even one who carries films—as some do— into the bush, feedback can influence only some future work that may be months or years away.

> Our history was not taught to people of my generation. We know the dates, the legends, but we don't clearly see what happened. Our aim . . . is to dramatize history and to teach it so as not to let others teach it to us.
>
> —Ousmane Sembene

The arguments for filmmaker as *griot* seem to be prescriptive: directors should assume this role to help preserve an African view of the past. As cultural strategy, this may be admirable, but what kind of history does it imply? Consider the most highly-regarded African filmmaker, Ousmane Sembene of Senegal. A self-conscious artist—as Françoise Pfaff makes clear in her book-length study—Sembene has claimed the role of *griot*, has aimed to become the "mouth and ears" of society, the one who "reflects and synthesizes the problems, the struggles, and the hopes of his people."[4] More regularly than any other African filmmaker, he has turned to the past as the setting for his films. This includes his masterpiece—perhaps the masterpiece of African cinema—*Ceddo*, a work that is at once an epic, a drama, a folk tale, a morality play, and a piece of history.

But not history as we normally know it in a book or on the screen. Not history that would dare begin with the claim "This is a true story." *Ceddo* brings together "bits and pieces of facts and authentic events that took place in a period spanning the centuries," and compresses them into a few days in the life of a single seventeenth-century village.[5] A few days jam-packed with action precipitated by a long-running conflict between a group of Muslims headed by a militant Imam and the devotees of the traditional tribal religion. Included are the following events: the kidnapping of a princess, the battles of warriors to redeem her, the death of a king (possibly by poisoning), the torching of homes, the slaughter of the innocent families, the rise to power of the Imam, the forced conversion of the tribal masses, and, finally—in a reassertion of tradition—the death of the Imam at the hands of the princess.

So many incidents packed into such a short period of time make for a film that can seem overtly fictional rather than historical. Its style heightens this feeling. To Western eyes, *Ceddo*—for all its events—seems slow, talky, awkward, "unrealistic." Why? Because it is free of Hollywood conventions. Because it is shot in what Pfaff calls African film language—a language that aims at a holistic portrait of people set within, and never separated from, their natural and human surroundings; a language that includes long sequences, minimal

editing, medium shots, and limited camera movement. *Ceddo* lacks closeups, matched sightlines, and
over-the-shoulder shots. For anyone conditioned by
Hollywood (all of us), the film also lacks intimacy,
identification with the characters, and emotional pull.
Here is an irony. The "realism" we miss in *Ceddo* de-
rives from its emotional distance; this same distance in
written history seems to guarantee a realism we call
"objectivity."

For the historian, the style of *Ceddo* may be less
upsetting than its contents. Can "history" be allowed
to conflate events from different times and places? Yet
how else could a filmmaker deal with the crucial
conflict between Islam and the native religions in West
Africa, or with any such conflict that took place over
centuries and about which few specifics of time and
place are known? Unlike words, film cannot deal with
abstract concepts, cannot generalize about things
which happen over time. The filmmaker must show
images on the screen, specific images. In choosing to
conflate events in order to create images for history,
Sembene may not give us a "true" story (one that
reflects what happened at some particular time in
some particular location) but a story that captures
(and creates) historical truth. *Ceddo* is thus the visual
equivalent of history as told by a *griot*. It is a work that
bypasses the written stage of history to transfer the
oral tradition, with its moral rather than chronological
truths, directly to the screen.

Because our history has been filtered through a bourgeois lens we have been compelled to live with terrible

distortions. We lack a coherent, lucid, and dignified appreciation of our national past.

—Humberto Solas

Like African filmmakers, Latin Americans have been deeply concerned with recapturing the image for themselves, with creating the conditions for cultural autonomy, with expressing a sense of "national reality." Yet they have differed from Africans in being (1) more overtly interested in questions of history on film and (2) more theoretical in their approach to cinema. Theory, in fact, has underwritten a good number of film movements since the sixties. The notion of a Third Cinema, enunciated in Argentina by Fernando Solanas and Octavio Getino, aimed at filmmaking that would privilege neither the producer (like Hollywood) nor the director (like European *auteur* cinema), but would "emphasize the interaction between film and audience in open, essay-style documentaries that would spur spectators to political action."[6] Movements that followed include Imperfect Cinema (rejecting of technical excellence), Cinema Rescate (recovering what was hidden), Cinema of Hunger, Cinema Novo, and—taken over from literature—Tropicalism, Cannibalism, and the Carnivalesque.

We cannot make films to express Brazilian or Latin American content using North American language.

—Glauber Rocha

The broad-ranging goals and doctrines of these new cinemas can be sampled in Julianne Burton's collection of well-conducted interviews, *Cinema and Social Change in Latin America*. Here directors, producers, and actors from Argentina, Bolivia, Brazil, Chile, and Cuba recount their ideas, hopes, dreams, successes, and failures with a kind of commitment, passion, and intellectual sophistication that—for those used to the mumblings of Hollywood directors and stars—can seem dazzling. Certain beliefs are held in common: that "official" history has distorted the past by suppressing evidence of racism, exploitation, resistance, and rebellion; that film must be used to change people's consciousness by teaching them the realities of both their heritage and their current situation; that a cinema necessary for a new consciousness must create its own language and filmic forms. These ideas underline a "double commitment" among Latin filmmakers—a commitment not just to "social transformation" but also to "artistic innovation."[7]

Social transformation was the easy part, at least as an ideal. All you needed was—in the words of Brazil's Glauber Rocha—"a camera in your hand and an idea in your head."[8] Along with a desire to cover topics, peoples, and problems that had been ignored in schoolbooks and shunned by middle-class politicians. In the sixties, youngsters began to leave the confines of their privileged urban worlds in order to seek out the poor and the dispossessed in city slums and remote backlands. To topics such as homeless children in Buenos Aires, brickmakers in Bogota, peasants in Bolivia, they brought a documentary approach. But with this major difference: to avoid the usual elitism of film practice, which turns subjects into passive objects of the camera, they would insist that their subjects collaborate in the creation of the film. Artistic innovation was and is a more difficult idea, both to describe in words and to put into practice. It enters the Latin cinema as part of the move from the documentary to the historical drama. Innovation is needed—the argument goes—because history as taught in every Latin country and the historical images created in Hollywood (and in Latin Hollywoods) are linked together by capitalism, consumerism, and the state. To recapture the hidden past, one cannot simply dramatize social history (topics such as slavery, the working class, peasants, or political resistance) in Hollywood-style films that will comfort the audience with a nice emotional release. One must, rather, jerk the audience out of its well-made dreams—out of the passive role of film consumer. And this can be done only by creating disturbing film forms and utilizing a new film language that will make historical issues vital, urgent, full of contemporary meaning.

> I didn't want to make a closed film that would permit only one reading.
>
> —Nelson Pereira dos Santos

Experiments in the historical film have been common in Latin America for twenty years now. Strategies for conveying the past have varied from realism to fantasy to the mixing of genres and forms. Some directors have achieved a gritty sort of "realism" by on-site reconstructions of events with the help of the original participants. The originator and specialist in this vein was Jorge Sanjinés; his first such work, *Courage of the*

People (1971), is a re-creation of a strike and massacre, scripted and acted by Bolivian miners. Other directors have—through long shots, stylized acting, and minimal editing—distanced the spectator from events on the screen, creating a (Brechtian) film world in which it is impossible to achieve close emotional identification with the characters. The master of this genre was Glauber Rocha (*Black God, White Devil,* 1963; *Antonio das Mortes,* 1969); his aim, to make people think about, rather than simply feel, the problems presented on the screen.

For many filmmakers, realism was not the solution but the problem. Some dreamed of an "open" film, a work that would leave the audience not with answers but questions. Easier said than done. Virtually all Latin historical films have been strongly anti-capitalist. (One person's openness is another's ideology!) Certainly this has been true in Cuba, where the regime has systematically sponsored historical films. (The background to this—along with the entire story of the politics and aesthetics of Cuban film from the first feature in 1913 through the 1970s—is detailed in Michael Chahan's comprehensive work, *The Cuban Image.*) Obviously, the aim in underwriting works of history has been to create a heritage and tradition for the values of the socialist regime (much as American historical films work to legitimate our values of freedom, individualism, democracy). But such a strategy could be pursued with any sort of motion picture. The real interest in Cuban film lies in its filmic experiments (no socialist realism here!). In these experiments, techniques that rupture the surface "realism" of the screen convey a sense of how past and present interpenetrate. Here are three good examples:

1. *Lucia* (Humberto Solas, 1968) consists of three episodes set in three periods (colonial, 1895; neocolonial, 1933; revolutionary, 1960s), each centered around a woman named Lucia (an aristocrat; a middle-class city girl; a peasant in a collective) whose problems with the political system and a man are conveyed in three different dramatic genres (tragedy, melodrama, comedy) and three visual styles (dark and tragic, shadowy and realistic, bright and playful). All underscore the notion that there is no single way to look at the past or to think about what history means.

2. *First Charge of the Machete* (Manuel Octavio Gomez, 1969) reconstructs a single battle against Spain in 1868 as a documentary. High-contrast film, jumpy images from hand-held cameras, direct sound, interviews with soldiers, and street scenes of people in Havana—all give the feeling of "events filmed as they occur." History told like this can be no "illusion of distant times," no "vehicle of escapism."[9] The form insists that the issues of history are as immediate as those of our own time.

3. *El Otro Francisco* (Sergio Giral, 1974) provides dual perspectives on a single subject. Based on Cuba's first antislavery novel (from the 1830s), the film dramatizes two views of slave life: one incorporates the romantic sensibility of the novel, the other reflects our current view of slavery as a horror. To see the nineteenth century through two sets of beliefs—those of

the reformers of the period (as reconstituted today)
and of contemporary Marxists (as constituted today)—is to confront the time-based nature of all historical knowledge.

> Cinema is not the reproduction of reality. It implies the
> creation of a parallel, alternative, and verisimilar uni-
> verse. This verisimilitude nourishes itself more on the
> spirit and ideology of the spectators than on their daily
> experience.
>
> —Carlos Diegues

More than any other Latin country, Brazil has been
fertile ground for new cinematic visions. It has also
been one of the few countries in which opposition
cinema has reached a general audience. The reason,
claim Randal Johnson and Robert Stam in the historical survey that introduces *Brazilian Cinema,* is that
filmmakers in Brazil have created movies that transcend the usual critical dichotomies, movies that are
at once radical and popular, didactic and frivolous—"a
synthesis of energy and consciousness, emotion and
dialectics, humor and political purpose."[10] The book's
theoretical statements and analyses of individual films
give a sense of a unique Brazilian vision—or series of
overlapping visions—referred to, variously, as Tropicalism, Cannibalism, the Carnivalesque. A vision that,
to "the stodginess of an alien European culture," op-
poses "the vitality of Brazilian popular culture"[11]: a
culture that emphasizes dance, music, food, bodily
functions, and laughter as positive historical forces. A
culture in which social and economic hierarchies are
inverted and, if only for a short time, the values of the

oppressed—blacks, Indians, women, the lower classes—reign supreme.

The vision seems especially marked in historical films. Tropicalism in the epic *Macunaima* (Joaquin Pedro de Andrade, 1969). Cannibalism in the "captive witness" tale *How Tasty Was My Little Frenchman* (Nelson Pereira dos Santos, 1970). And the Carnivalesque in two works by Carlos Diegues dealing with black slavery, *Xica de Silva* (1976) and *Quilombo* (1984). Banquets, dancing, and seduction mark the former film, a chronicle of role reversals that stem from the actions of a freed slave who uses her erotic powers to dominate the leading men—and through them the politics and economics—of the eighteenth-century state of Minas Gerais. The latter work carries both the theme of black power and the feeling of Carnival onto a broader canvas. The subject is the history of Palmares, the most long-lived of Brazil's many republics of runaway slaves. Here it is a republic of theater, a realm of fantastic costumes, painted faces and bodies, continual music, and dance—including the samba. Anachronistic—definitely. But realism is hardly the aim. In the absence of detailed knowledge of actual life in Palmares, *Quilombo* glorifies a tribal culture freed from the burden of Christian civilization. It gives us history that chronicles not material forms but the spirit of the past.

> Never before and in no other country have images and languages been handled as unscrupulously as here, never before and in no other place have they been so debased as vehicles for lies.
>
> —Wim Wenders

Love-hate. Toward their own (Nazi) past and toward Hollywood. That's the double burden of German filmmakers. If the animus toward Hollywood seems surprising, remember: Germans since 1945 have lived in an occupied country, at least in the realm of popular culture. "The Yankees have even colonized our subconscious," says a character who is mindlessly humming an American pop song in *Kings of the Road* (1976).[12] For those who created the New German Cinema in the sixties and seventies, Hollywood presented a dual face: its slick products seemed to offer a kind of redemption through technical proficiency; its relentlessly bright images and brighter message ("Let's have a happy ending every time") were alien to the German experience. Yet not more alien than the messages in their own cinema: German film in the postwar era was a dream world full of nostalgic stories of star-crossed lovers, family problems set in an idealized small-town Germany, war tales that focused on the heroism of common soldiers. The painful truths of the recent past, the complexities and complicities of German history—were ignored or repressed.

The psychic, economic, and political results of occupation; the struggle against an internalized Hollywood; the way in which filmmakers have sought to recover (or redefine) a national identity through the language, the form, the subject matter of their works—all these topics are deftly treated in Tim Corrigan's book, *New German Film*. Of those directors whose films receive extended readings (Wim Wenders, Rainer Werner Fassbinder, Volker Schlöndorff, Alexander Kluge, Werner Herzog), none is more outspoken against cinematic imperialism than Hans Jürgen Syberberg. "War" is his cry. War against "Hollywood and its satellites." War against "psychological chitchat, against the action film, against a particular philosophy of endlessly linking shots and reverse shots . . . against the melodrama of crime and sex."[13]

The psychic, economic, and political results of a history that has been repressed; the struggle to fill a historical vacuum; the way in which filmmakers have sought to recover (or redefine) a national past through the language, the form, the subject matter of their works—all this is treated in Anton Kaes's book *From Hitler to Heimat*. (And treated with a rare blend of historical understanding and critical insight that make this the finest single work to date on the relationship between film and history.) The focus is films by five directors, films that deal with major historical topics: Hitler, the Holocaust, and German identity. These films are so serious about historical questions that "they prefigure by several years . . . current revisionist attempts by Germans to come to terms with their past—a past that will not go away precisely because its representations are everywhere."[14]

> That our history is in everything of necessity our most important heritage, both for good and evil, is the fate laid upon us at birth, and something we can only work our way through with an active effort.
>
> —Hans Jürgen Syberberg

How to "work through" a history so terrible, so physically and psychically devastating? How to overcome the powerful legacy of Nazi film, the distrust of all images and sounds dealing with Germany? Traditional stories and forms do for some filmmakers: Fassbinder in the rags-to-riches tale *The Marriage of Maria Braun* (1978); Helma Sanders-Brahms in the autobiographical *Germany, Pale Mother* (1980); and Edgar Reitz in the sixteen-hour saga of small-town life *Heimat* (1984). Others feel the need to handle historical extremes with extremes of invention, an unprecedented past with unprecedented forms of film. Among them, Hans Jürgen Syberberg and Alexander Kluge are the most ambitious and inventive. More than dealing with a legacy of Nazism, their works propose new ways of visualizing the past.

Syberberg's concern is with myths—with destroying the negative ones to restore the positive. His focus is the largest myth of all: Adolf Hitler. A figure too large for "realism" to contain; a figure who has long since "dissolved into a plurality of images."[15] In six hours and forty-five minutes of *Hitler, a Film from Germany* (1977) there is no historical footage: none of the familiar scenes of strutting storm troopers, Nuremberg rallies, Panzer divisions. Such images imply a reality to be mirrored, but past reality is gone and these sorts of filmic reflections are essentially lies, for they both take the place of and conceal all the unfilmable and unfilmed events and realities that make up the past. It is more honest to create history on a stage in a studio (much as historians create it in their studies). And create Syberberg does, in a multitextured work of juxtaposition and contradiction, a bewildering pastiche of dramatic forms whose power words cannot convey. Puppets and actors in monologues and sketches; blatant anachronisms (Hitler praises those who continue his work today); overlays of speeches, pop music, and opera—all create history "as a circus and amusement park, as a horror cabinet, a puppet theater, as a cabaret and side show, as tribunal, Grand Guignol, and commedia dell'arte . . ."[16]

> We must begin work on our history. I mean something very concrete by that; we could even start by telling each other stories.
>
> —Alexander Kluge

Digging for the past is easy. Making it mean something is much more difficult. What you come up with are disconnected fragments that do not fit together into a complete and meaningful story. That's the problem both for Kluge and for the history teacher who is central to his film *Die Patriotin* (1979). Like the director, the teacher is involved in researching two thousand years of German history. Eventually she digs up so many contradictory things that she can no longer make sense of them. Neither can Kluge. So rather than give the audience a unified story, he provides fragments of the past and hopes that we will assemble them. Two things complicate our task: (1) In *Die Patriotin* fact and fiction interpenetrate: the actress playing the teacher appears, for example, in documentary footage at a meeting of the Christian Democratic Party, where she interviews delegates, who think she is a teacher, not an actress, about German history. (2) The world of the past in the film is a nonlinear mixture of heterogeneous texts: images (photos, film clips, illustrations); odd facts from everyday life (the price of geese in Silesia in 1914); references to products of the imagination (Grimms' fairy tales, comic strips); and quotations from the history of music, painting, and film.

Difficult, yes. A jumble, no. There is a method here, a technique for doing history that we may call "nomadic and analytic." Two thousand years—Kluge insists—cannot be grasped from a single perspective or compressed into a single story. Historical knowledge has splintered, disintegrated. The only honest way for us to render the fullness of the past is through montage, the juxtaposition of unlike images to form new combinations of meaning—a meaning that we, the viewers, must work to achieve. The search of the director and of his character is our search too. The way around "official" history is to undertake history as an open form, to show the process by which we construct the past. To make, in fact, the process by which history produces meaning part of the meaning produced. To insist: "Only if the reconstruction of the past itself is made the object of inquiry can the past be seen in a critical light."[17]

> Cinema has not changed the world, but the way of understanding the world in this century.
> —Carlos Diegues

Who speaks for the past? And in what medium? And by what rules? Such questions are bound to arise from any encounter with experiments in history on film.

They are questions to keep in mind as we attempt to evaluate the possibilities of visual history. One thing is certain: the history on film done in Africa, Latin America, and Germany is far more serious in both intent and result than that done in Hollywood. So serious that, as we have seen, many filmmakers have found it necessary to shatter the traditional narrative forms of the medium in order to explore the relationship of the past to the present. In the realm of cinema, the accomplishments of those mentioned here—their contributions to the language, form, and history of the medium—are secure. But what about their contribution to history? None of the authors of these books is a historian. All are based in literary or film studies. However interested they are in the relationship of film to the past, none has the particular concerns of the historian.

The issues raised by these different works of visual history are more complex than those raised by the typical illusionist, realist drama. For that sort of film, the basic questions are: Is it true? How much has been invented? But the oral historical approach of *Ceddo*, the Tropicalist works of Brazil, the postmodern constructions of Syberberg and Kluge call forth larger questions. Perhaps impossible questions: What is historical truth? How can we show it? Does it depend upon cultural context? Upon the era? Upon the medium? None of these can be answered easily, or by an appeal to "facts." Any answers involve matters of social, cultural, and personal politics and values. They include our (individual and collective) aims in wanting to do history in the first place, the kind of history we do, the historical questions we want answered, the social position from which we write.

History on film—particularly in these innovative works—is history (literally and metaphorically) as vision. As vision (of a culture, an era, a civilization) that precedes any notion of "fact." As vision that calls "facts" into being by providing a framework in which they make sense. To call such films visions is not to exclude them from the realm of criticism. But it is to insist that judgments about them not be made with criteria inappropriate to their aims. Collectively, these films point to gaps in our understanding of the past. All highlight the fact that we do not yet know how to judge a historical work that refuses literalism as its presentational mode. Yet such literalism is a convention which, like all conventions, has marked limits. For certain events or periods of the past—plagues, warfare, terror, concentration camps—literalism may create a feeling of normality, when the true feelings we wish to convey might call out for "facts" delivered through an expressionist or surrealist mode of presentation.

Even without well-developed criteria of judgment, we can see that each sort of film has potential problems and dangers as a vehicle of history. It is possible that, in their emphasis on the *griot,* Africans may be flogging a dead tradition. What, one may ask, is the use of carrying on oral history in a modern electronic society? Some Latin Americans may seem to be overly political, doctrinaire Marxists in a world where Marxism as a form of social organization is clearly on the decline. German directors can appear to be so interested in the razzle-dazzle of postmodern fragmentation that certain moral questions are too easily ignored. One has at least to wonder at the strategies of many recent German films which focus on the suffering of the German people during the Second World War, but never depict the Jewish, Polish, and Gypsy victims of the Holocaust.

Some may wish to argue that ideology—tribal, Marxist, national—is at the heart of the films mentioned here. (One can just as easily see ideology at the heart of the "illusionist" Hollywood film. Or, for that matter, at the heart of our positivist or hermeneutical written historical projects.) But it is important to see that these new sorts of history on film can transcend particular ideologies. Once created, certain techniques and forms may be separated both from the culture in which they were invented and from the ideological messages of particular works and then used in other contexts. The *griot* may be African, but tellers of historical tales are widespread. Tropicalism may seem particularly Brazilian, but an emphasis on song and dance marks other parts of the world. Postmodernism can be found around the globe. One of its most brilliant examples as history is the 1987 film *Walker,* which uses deliberate anachronisms, humor, and overt absurdity both to portray the adventurer who became president of Nicaragua in the 1850s and to comment on America's long-running interventionism in that land.

The various experiments in historical film provide a series of challenges to visual and to written history. They test the boundaries of what we can say about the past and how we can say it. They point to the limitations of conventional historical form. They suggest other ways to envision the past. They make us think about how the past means to us. About why we study it. About what we want from it. They challenge written history by showing how our literary forms are limited by the notions of "realism" and "literalism." Yet for all these challenges, it is difficult to say exactly how such experimental visions fit into our larger sense of history. Perhaps—like memory, like oral history—they will simply exist in a historical world adjacent to the written one. Perhaps they will give us another sort of past to live with. Or perhaps they will change the way traditional historians—and some members of the public—think about the past.

For historians who work in words, the experimental history on film may seem outlandish, bizarre, simply beyond the pale. History as carnival? Admit that and where do you draw the line? Such a question cannot yet be answered, not until more people who care about history come to grips with an expanded notion of the historical film. Taken together, the new visual histories provide a cautionary note for both partisans and opponents of the visual media. Yes—they say—history on film can be far more interesting and serious (and useful) than history in the normal Hollywood film. But it is not history in the sense that academics think of it. It is history with different rules of representation and analysis, and modes of reading and comprehension—rules we don't yet fully understand. After confronting these works, one has to know that history on film can be intellectually complex, challenging, and demanding. But it is still impossible to know to what extent historians—or other academics—will credit such visual knowledge. Ultimately the question comes down to this: To what extent can we let the "truths" of visual history be our "truths"? Which means: To what extent will we insist that the concept of historical "truth" can be encoded only in the written word? No matter how we academics answer this, the historical film will continue to play a role in the way we see, remember, think about, and understand the past.

· 9 ·

Film and the Beginnings of Postmodern History

Among the many written forms of history, we can distinguish a spectrum that runs from the popular to the scholarly, from those works intended for a "general" audience to those aimed at specialists. A similar spectrum marks the historical film, which goes from the multi-million-dollar Hollywood epic like Schindler's List, *to the tiny-budget, grant-dependent individual work, sometimes shot on video, that may only be screened only at specialized festivals. Like popular history, the Hollywood film (and the miniseries, its television counterpart) aims at the broadest of mass audiences with conventions of drama and character that are easy to understand. More interesting visually, conceptually, and also as history is the small, personal kind of film dealt with in this article. An odd counterpart to serious scholarship (at least in the limited nature of its audience), these historical films, which fulfill the postmodern agenda of some theorists, expand our sense of history by allowing us to see our relationship to the past in new and interesting ways.*

Thesis: The argument of this (sketch for an) essay can be stated simply: among theorists of and apologists for postmodernism (the two categories overlap), there are a few who take time to discuss a new kind of historical writing—a postmodern history which, apparently, brings the way we know or think of the past into line with the poststructuralist critique of current historical practice. As examples of this tendency, these theorists point toward the work of certain historians, or to particular genres of historical writing, or to individual works of history. But something odd happens between the notions of postmodern history and its exemplars, for as any fool can plainly see (as my father would have said), the historians, genres, and works of history named do not really fulfill the notions of postmodernism as outlined by these theorists themselves. Works that fulfill their notions of this new kind of history do exist, but not at all where the theorists are pointing. For while professional historians continue, with but a tiny number of exceptions, to write in a highly traditional manner, a variety of little-known filmmakers and videographers have begun to create a kind of history that we can label truly postmodern, producing works that provide a distinctly new relationship to and a new way of making meaning of the traces of the past.[1]

Confession: Pardon the digression, but I feel the need to explain that I come to this issue not as a theorist (you can tell that already), but as a historian. One trained some thirty years ago in the Dragnet school of history—Just the facts, ma'am. Intellectual developments in the quarter century since then—the poststructuralist revolution—have clearly altered my beliefs, but not wholly destroyed them. Even if I now know that we historians constitute our objects of study on the basis of ideological and political agendas, and create narratives (or even analytic articles) shaped not by data but by linguistic rules and prefigured tropes, I still believe we have something important to learn from studying long-gone people, beliefs, moments, movements, and events (yes, we need these, too). So if my faith in the truth of what we can know about the past has diminished, my need for such knowledge remains firm. From Dragnet history I have moved on to Samuel Beckett history—I can't go on, I'll go on.

Postmodern History? The notion of postmodern history seems like a contradiction in terms. The heart of postmodernism, all theorists agree, is a struggle against History. With a capital *H*. A denial of its narratives, findings, and truth claims. A view of it as the great enemy, the oedipal father, the metanarrative of metanarratives, the last and greatest of the white mythologies used to legitimate Western hegemony, a false and outworn discourse that fosters nationalism, racism, ethnocentrism, colonialism, sexism—and all the other evils of contemporary society.

One (unusually) clear statement of the case against history has postmodernism questioning: *(1) the idea that there is a real, knowable past, a record of evolutionary progress of human ideas, institutions, or actions, (2) the view that historians should be objective, (3) that reason enables historians to explain the past, and (4) that the role of history is to interpret and transmit human cultural and intellectual tradition from generation to generation.*[2]

Surprise! Nonetheless: a few theorists of postmodernism display a certain amount of interest in, even sympathy for, a study of the past—for doing history with a small *h*. Among them are Linda Hutcheon, Elizabeth Deeds Ermarth, Pauline Rosenau, F. R. Ankersmit, and Hans Kellner. It will violate their individual views to do so, but let me present a kind of pastiche, taken from their writings, that describes the history they admire:

History that *problematizes the entire notion of historical knowledge.* That foregrounds the *usually concealed attitude of historians toward their material.* That reeks with *provisionality and undecidability, partisanship and even overt politics.* That *engages pulse and intellect simultaneously.* That *breaks down the convention of historical time and substitutes a new convention of temporality—rhythmic time.* That does not aim at *integration, synthesis, and totality.* That is content with *historical scraps.* That is not *the reconstruction of what has happened to us in the various phases of our lives, but a continuous playing with the memory of this.* That is expressed not in coherent stories but in *fragments* and *collage.*[3]

One Oddity: When these theorists attempt to cite examples of postmodern history, they tend to wave in the direction of categories and genres instead of dealing with the specific works.

Example: For Linda Hutcheon, *postmodern* or *New* history (she elides the terms, as do others) includes a wide range of approaches, from the *Annales* school to histories that highlight the past experiences of the formerly excluded: women, ethnic minorities, gays, losers (rather than winners), regional and colonial peoples, and the many (rather than the few, or the ruling elites).[4]

Example: Pauline Marie Rosenau sees postmodern— or New—history as employing *deconstruction, subjective interpretation, and a symbolic construction of reality, rather than quantitative, structural, or functional methods . . . it seeks to unravel texts, raise questions about meaning in the text, and invent micro-narratives as alternatives to history.* Her list of genres points to works written by feminist, African-American, new-Marxist, psychoanalytic, and *discourse-oriented* historians.[5]

Another Oddity: When these theorists attempt to name individual historians responsible for works of post-modern history, they point toward two kinds of scholars: (1) Other theorists. People like themselves who do not (apparently) deal with the *pulse* of the past at all. That is, historians who ignore textualized events, movements, individuals, in order to analyze textualized texts, works of high culture, the writings of philosophers, critics, and historians. The common names given: Hayden White, Dominick La Capra, Jacques Derrida, Michel Foucault. (2) Fairly traditional historians who have broadened the discipline by approaching topics with tools drawn from other disciplines, especially anthropology, literature, philosophy, critical theory, and gender studies. Or who have helped to open up new subject areas—working class, ethnic, feminist, subaltern, gay. The common names, mentioned repeatedly: Emmanuel Le Roy Ladurie, Georges Duby, Carlo Ginzburg, Natalie Davis.

A Third Oddity: When these same theorists attempt to name actual works of postmodern history, they provide a (very) few titles, over and over: Emmanuel Le Roy Ladurie, *Montaillou;* Natalie Davis, *The Return of Martin Guerre;* Carlo Ginzburg, *The Cheese and the Worms.*

A Fourth: Opponents of postmodernism take the same slash-and-burn approach. In a piece entitled *Telling it as you like it: Post-modernist history and the flight from fact,* the most outspoken of them, Gertrude Himmelfarb, has great difficulty in actually locating examples of the new kind of history she trashes with such ferocious glee.[6] Denouncing both Joan Scott and Theodore Zeldin without ever mentioning their actual historical works,[7] she points to a single example of postmodern history—Simon Schama's *Dead Certainties,* a book comprised of what the author calls two *novellas . . . works of the imagination, not scholarship.*[8] Clearly, specificity is much less fun than soundly thrashing the *usual suspects:* White, La Capra, Foucault, and Derrida.

Borgesian History? Hutcheon and Rosenau, Himmelfarb, and the other theorists have apparently forgotten only the kitchen sink. Maybe it won't fit in their conceptually overstuffed grab bags. The problem is that the lists of genres, historians, and works of history are oddly unparallel, largely mistaken, curiously unrevealing, and highly self-contradictory. The *Annales* (named by Hutcheon) began (and continues) as an attempt to make history more scientific, not more problematic; to this day, *Annales* historians are likely to call themselves scientists rather than humanists. As for the formerly excluded (named by all theorists)— whether one points to subject matter (ethnics, gays, colonials) or approach (psychoanalytic, neo-Marxist), at least two things must be said: (1) Many of the categories (African-Americans, the working class) and approaches (say neo-Marxism) are not new, but have been part of traditional history for decades now, and are an accepted part of historical discourse. (2) Other categories (losers, or regionals, or colonials) may be considered outsiders only from certain standpoints—it is increasingly recognized by historians now that one person's margins are always someone else's center. For a historian of India, Senegal, or Viet Nam, Western Europe can now be considered the periphery.

The Point: The historians, the genres, and the individual works mentioned by theorists who discuss works of history do not at all fulfill their own critique of traditional history or the notions of postmodern history that they elaborate.

This is not to deny that in the past quarter century, historians have opened up vast new areas of study (pointed to by the theorists) and created many new approaches for excavating and rethinking the remains of the past—indeed, the achievements of the New Social history, and of feminists and postcolonial historians, in giving voice to those previously voiceless (women, ethnic minorities, industrial workers, peasants, the colonized) are so extensive and well-known that one can hardly remember a time when they were not part of our historical picture. But in their presentations of the past, in the way they write, these historians have not strayed from very traditional notions of realistic narrative, logical explanation, linear argument, traditional cause and effect. Indeed, so tame is their prose that one has to wonder whether the theorists have actually read the historical works they label postmodern. (What one suspects, of course, is that they ignore works of history in favor of reading other theorists.)

Emmanuel Le Roy Ladurie's *Montaillou*, in which multiple voices speak with and interpenetrate that of the historian, may be the single work of history to move any real distance toward formal literary innovation. None of the other scholars cited goes so far. None (including Le Roy Ladurie) uses pastiche or collage. None creates a world that includes new notions of temporality, such as rhythmic time. None problematizes major assertions. None presents a world comprised of scraps, or gives up traditional modes of analysis. And when these histories foreground the politics and ideology of the author, the do so in the preface—just where historians have always felt free to bare their souls and ideologies.[9]

The examples of the so-called postmodern history touted by the theorists are, to anyone who has a taste for the new, a real disappointment. Certainly they have nothing in common with the postmodernism exhibited in other fields and art forms. These histories contain none of the dash, the humor, the mixing of genres, the pastiche, the collage, the odd juxtapositions, the temporal jumps, the wacky illogic of the architecture, theater, or literature we label postmodern. Ultimately they seem to fill nobody's notions of the postmodern—not the theorists, not mine, and not—may I assume?—yours.

Filmmakers to the Rescue: If you long for new kinds of history, if you think we need new ways of relating to the past, don't despair. Postmodern history has been born and is currently alive and well. It exists not on the page but on the screen, and is the creation of filmmakers and videographers. By both traditional and modern standards, this should not be surprising. The visual media have become our chief means of telling each other about the world. And filmmakers clearly have much less stake in traditional ways of rendering the past than do historians—though they have no less stake in its meaning.

What do these (real) postmodern history films do to the past? Lots of things: (1) Tell the past self-reflexively, in terms of how it means to the filmmaker historian. (2) Recount it from a multiplicity of viewpoints. (3) Eschew traditional narrative, with its beginning, middle, and end—or, following Jean-Luc Godard, insist these three elements need not necessarily be in that order. (4) Forsake normal story development, or tell stories but refuse to take the telling seriously. (5) Approach the past with humor, parody, and absurdist, surrealist, dadaesque, and other irreverent attitudes. (6) Intermix contradictory elements—past and present, drama and documentary—and indulge in creative anachronism. (7) Accept, even glory in, their own selectivity, partialism, partisanship, and rhetorical character. (8) Refuse to focus or sum up the meaning of past events, but instead make sense of them in a partial and open-ended, rather than totalized, manner. (9) Alter and invent incident and character. (10) Utilize fragmentary or poetic knowledge. (11) Never forget that the present is the site of all past representation and knowing.

To exemplify how such elements are used, I shall move to some descriptions of postmodern history films, doing so in the full knowledge that these descriptions should be not on a page but on a screen—as film or video or, better yet, as an interactive CD-ROM that mixes text, moving image, and sound, or over the Internet, with moving visual images and text. These media are, I think, uniquely capable of dealing with the multiple, complex, and overlapping elements that comprise historical film. At least one work of history and one in cinema studies have appeared on or utilized CD-ROM.[10] A few years from now, articles on the visual media will appear routinely in such formats. But at this moment, even as I write in a style designed to shake up normal academic forms and expectations and to approximate, however distantly, the cuts and juxtapositions of the visual media, I must confess to being hyper-aware of the difficulties and limitations of describing films in words—especially obscure films that you, the reader, may not have seen. This means you will have to trust me even more than you usually trust the author of a scholarly essay. A similar problem of trust is posed by the historical film, pre- or post-modern. Because films lack footnotes, bibliography, and other scholarly apparatus, they have difficulty justifying the accuracy of their vision of the past to the audience. The usual strategy is to overwhelm you with drama, color, sound. Mine is to disarm you with this confession. But take heed: before you accept my arguments, go get these films and see them for yourself.

Welcome to the Show: With something as new as post-modern history, division into smaller categories seems premature. Yet to show the range and diversity of such films, I shall describe works that, were they written pieces of history, might well fall into such widely recognized categories as contemporary, ethnic, national, cultural, gender, and comparative history.

Contemporary: Jill Godmilow's *Far from Poland* (1984), shot at the beginning of the Solidarity movement, deals with a contemporary topic in a self-reflexive way—foregrounding the life of the filmmaker in order to show how personal matters affect both the film and the history of Solidarity that it renders: a history—like almost all works of history—created a great distance away in time or space from the events it analyzes.

Far from Poland begins with the filmmaker talking

from note cards directly into the camera. Explaining that she happened to be in Poland when the shipyard strikes began in Gdansk in 1980, Godmilow tells us that she flew back to New York, raised some money, hired a camera crew, and bought tickets for Warsaw. Her aim: *to tell the real story.* Godmilow's image is replaced by that of a worker with a helmet and blowtorch who says: *Let me tell you a story.* His tale is not, as we might expect, about the shipyards, but about a documentary filmmaker, steeped in the traditions of the left, who *searched the world for the face of humanity* and found it in Poland at the time of the strikes. The camera pulls back and we see that the worker's image is on a video monitor in an editing room, with Godmilow watching it and groaning. In voiceover, she tells us that this is her current friend, Mark Magill, a performance artist whose notion of Marxism is of the *Harpo, Zeppo variety.* The real Mark enters through a door and they argue over the film she is making: she talks about the struggles for truth and justice; he claims that, like everyone else, she only wants to use Solidarity to prove her ideas are right.

The competing voices in this opening sequence continue; the debate over what this work of history can mean grows ever more urgent as other voices join in. Once the filmmaker learns she cannot get a visa for Poland and decides to make a film anyway, in New York, her quandary over how to deal with Solidarity becomes part of the history she tells. The variety of methods she uses to present this history are inventive: along with the filmmaker's domestic drama and direct address, *Far from Poland* utilizes American TV footage, video shot for Godmilow by Solidarity cameramen, reenactments of interviews with workers that were published in the Polish press, interviews with Polish emigrés, letters from a friend in Poland, flashcards, midnight conversations (the screen is black) of Godmilow with Fidel Castro over the meaning of Socialism, a laugh track, and outtakes from a fictional movie, ostensibly shot by the famed director Andrzej Wajda in 1988 (four years after *Far from Poland* was released), showing the Polish dictator Wojciech Jaruzelski living under house arrest imposed by a new people's government which has succeeded his regime.

What sort of history does all this make? Godmilow not only learns, while making the film, that she cannot tell the real story: she also learns why nobody else can tell it either—for there is no real story to tell, but only a series of ways of representing, thinking about, and looking at the Polish movement. Yet for all the open admission of the personal stake of the filmmaker-historian in the outcome of the work, and the problematics of representation and knowledge that the film underlines, *Far from Poland* ends by making strong claims for the importance of the history of Solidarity (about which we do learn a good deal). The film suggests Solidarity is a highly significant human and social movement, a harbinger of change for Poland—and, perhaps, for other parts of Europe and the world. Not a bad prediction for a work which refuses to take itself absolutely seriously.[11]

▼ ▼ ▼

Ethnic: Rea Tajiri's *History and Memory* (1991) is also self-reflexive, but this video about the American relocation camps for Japanese Americans and Japanese during World War II foregrounds the personal stakes of the historian in uncovering the past. Early in the film, Tajiri tells us in voiceover, *I began searching for a history, my own history, because I knew the stories I had heard were not true—and parts of them had been left out,* while on the screen we see a woman, her back to the camera, standing in a dusty place and filling a canteen with water. This vision of her mother is Tajiri's sole legacy from the camps, a place she has never been but which she somehow can remember, a place of *great sadness* that has haunted her life.

Tajiri's desire to understand that single image fuels the film. Her problem of how to create a usable past that will ease the personal pain that history has caused is a double one: she must find a way around both social and personal amnesia—combat the lies, evasions, and partialisms of official history and the popular media, and get past the silence of the older generation of Japanese Americans about the camp experience (made literal in Tajiri's case by her mother's inability to remember anything at all).

In its resurrection of the past, *History and Memory* uses a good deal of the kind of archival film to be found in current documentaries. The film includes Japanese and American military footage of the attack on Pearl Harbor, clips from Hollywood films like *From Here to Eternity, Bad Day at Black Rock,* and *Come See the Paradise,* newsreels that show Japanese Americans going off to relocation centers, Office of War Information propaganda films about the necessity for the camps and the happiness of the internees, interviews with relatives who were incarcerated, footage of the filmmaker's personal journey to Poston, Arizona, where her family was held, and sequences from some illegally shot 8 mm footage of daily life in the camps (cameras were banned). It also includes some elements less common in documentary: dramatic reenactments of family scenes and, perhaps most unusual, a black screen with text scrolling over it to "show" us those important events that take place while no camera is watching—such as the condemnation and removal of her family's house by a government agency.

The structure that holds together the images and voices of *History and Memory* is not a traditional linear telling of the past, nor is the message a simple condemnation of the official racism sanctioned by war. Certainly the work contains enough information to give us a sense of the dimensions of the great injustice done to one group of Americans, and after a half century, the hyper-patriotic and feverish distortions of the media are starkly revealed. But the filmmaker's purpose goes beyond recapturing the past and redressing grievances. *History and Memory* is a work that creates a different notion of the past in its insistence that fact, fiction, and memory—including their distortions—are equally important elements of historical discourse.[12]

National: Ross Gibson's *Camera Natura* (1986) looks at the history of Australia from the earliest convict settlements to the present—but not in the way national histories are traditionally told. In this work there is nothing about economic development, social change, and political reform, for Gibson sees his country's history in terms of the relationship between the European population and the continent's landscape—as it has been depicted and imagined. The vast, inhospitable, and often intractable terrain has been central to the construction of the nation's mythologies and ideologies, to notions of Australian *character* and *destiny.*

Early in the film, we see a reenactment of an incident from the life of Tom Watling, an eighteenth-century transported convict and artist who was given the job of creating paintings that would transform the harsh landscape into something tame and homey for the audience back in Britain. Before doing his first work, Watling says directly to the camera, *I know what I'm supposed to do;* then we see the strokes he uses to soften and prettify the scene before him. For the filmmaker, Watling clearly is the traditional historian, molding the past to our comfortable expectations of neat and tidy progress. Overtly disdaining this approach to the past, *Camera Natura* goes on to create a far more elusive and disturbing kind of history.

What we see is a history composed of fragments assembled into a work that takes neither linear, cyclical, dialectical, or any other discernable form. The film moves backward and forward in time, ranging over the landscape (literally and figuratively) of past and present with a vast array of materials: maps, paintings, clips from fiction films and military documentaries, TV advertisements, dramatic recreations. Points are made not through linear or clear argument; instead one senses the themes: the land as threat and the land as spiritual inspiration; the wilderness as the foundation of both community and individualism; the evolution of the media—from eighteenth-century painting to nineteenth-century photography to twentieth-century moving images—as both the reflection and cause of historical change. Eros is present too, often in sublimated form. *Women and the earth,* proclaims a hero in the film: *I've always felt they were much the same, only the earth more exciting.* There is also an ongoing affair with changing modes of transportation—recurrent images of the horses, cars, and airplanes necessary to conquer the vast spaces of the continent.

The fragmentation that shatters the surface of *Camera Natura* is not the only aspect that marks it as postmodern. Most unusual for a work of history, particularly a national history, is its refusal of closure, an unwillingness to conclude that two hundred years of Australia add up to some notion or cluster of notions that are particularly good or bad for residents of the land. The final image of the work, a TV advertisement for fast food that shows sacred mountains suddenly transformed into a hamburger and french fries, may suggest something about the processes of secularization and commodification in the contemporary world—but the image, like many of the other images in this work, consciously creates an interpretive challenge for anyone wishing to understand the Australian past.[13]

▾ ▾ ▾

Cultural: Juan Downey's *Hard Times and Culture* (1990) views its much-studied subject, fin de siècle Vienna, from a contemporary point of view. The first image is of New York skyscrapers, while rappers on the soundtrack repeat a quotation from George Kubler: *An epoch of staggering difficulties above which painting, poetry and the theater flowered imperishably.* An African-American woman speaks to us on screen: *Out of the cesspool beautiful flowers come out of there, you know?* A cab driver looks in a rearview mirror—and sees Vienna at the time of Franz Josef.

The history that follows is as offbeat as the film's opening. Or perhaps one should say histories, for several approaches to the past jostle each other in this work. Politics comes to us in three ways: as waltz, as soap opera, as bad TV drama. A narrator tells us: *Like a waltz, the history of the empire can be played in triple meter, in three beats.* Each beat represents a death in the royal family—the murder of Empress Elisabeth, the suicide of Prince Rudolf at Mayerling, and the assassination of Archduke Franz Ferdinand and his wife at Sarajevo. Framed by a stylized TV screen, each death is presented in a factual but highly theatrical and melodramatic manner, with stage blood oozing and actors intoning fatuous (but sometimes historically documentable) lines: *Sophie, Sophie,* cries Franz Ferdinand, *don't die. Stay alive for the children.*

The undermining of traditional fact by juxtaposition, framing, and mode of presentation is a strategy pursued into the all-important (for Vienna) realm of culture. Indeed the relationship of data to interpretation is often vague. We hear lectures on the instability of the empire from a professorial type shakily riding a bike around the Ringstrasse; we learn that the Emperor maintained a box at every theater in the realm but never attended a single performance; we hear that Anton Bruckner had a *counting disease* that drove him to the edge of insanity while we see a billboard in America counting the mounting national debt; we see decadent Gustav Klimt portraits and learn they were painted for the newly rich; we look at Sigmund Freud's consultation room; we see a reenactment of Hugo von Hofmannsthal's work about Lord Chandos, a writer for whom language had lost its meaning. Such scenes are intercut with images from America—homeless people in New York, the African-American woman lecturing on the exploitation of black musicians, newspaper headlines from the Gulf War, tracking shots in a cemetery while dogs bark out the Death March.

The ordering of all this material may seem random, but the collective impact of image and sound is difficult to escape: assassination, suicide, political stagnation; the closeness of war; the divorce of the practical from the cultural; the obsession with numbers and objectivity; the increasing inability to communicate through shared language; the retreat into commercialism, the unconscious, silence—sound familiar? *Hard Times and Culture* is not the first work of history meant to function as a critique of the present, and certainly not the first to insist that the past has a great deal to teach us about where we stand in our political and cultural life. Indeed, for all the work's visual and verbal pyrotechnics, its aim may be seen as almost conventional. When its narrator tells us at the close that in Vienna *modernism* was not aimed toward the future but was, rather, an attempt to understand the past by *establishing the conditions that render the present possible,* the remark is self-referential—but to grasp those conditions in terms of today's consciousness, one must use, as Downey's film suggests, new and different modes of representation.[14]

Gender—Comparative: Trinh T. Minh-ha's *Surname Viet Given Name Nam* (1989), no doubt the best-known of the films described here, is a work that both delivers a history of Vietnamese women, at home and in the United States since the mid-seventies, and continually works to problematize its own assertions. The basic strategy becomes clear only halfway through the film when the viewer learns that the women apparently interviewed in Viet Nam during the first half of the film were actually Vietnamese women living in America who have been acting out interviews from published texts. To make matters more complex, the women, when in Viet Nam, speak heavily accented, sometimes unintelligible English, but playing themselves in America they speak subtitled Vietnamese.

Surrounding the interviews of women telling their lives are stories and ruminations, spoke in the filmmaker's voice, about women in Vietnamese history, along with footage of traditional dances, religious ceremonies, street scenes, markets, women at work, and poetic images of countryside, boats, and rivers. The sum of this material is a historical argument at once anti-patriarchal and anti-Confucian, an argument carried out in terms of both form and content. The film is not structured like the documentary developed in patriarchal society—linear, self-assured, omniscient. The form of its history is that of the women's dance which is the first image we see, a dance of patterns that recur but are never exactly the same. There is a paradox here, one that the filmmaker refuses to resolve. In its structure the work both insists on timelessness as a female characteristic and yet repeatedly shows how specific events (the war, migration) drastically change the contours and possibilities of women's lives.

To say *Surname Viet Given Name Nam* delivers a history is to redefine the term—but that surely is one of the points of a film in which the director herself, speaking over images of masses of marching women while we hear a train whistle blow (the engine of history?), says: *There is always a tendency to find historical breaks, to say this begins here and ends there, while the scene keeps recurring: as unchangeable as change itself.* And yet I would argue that, for all its attacks on common notions of historical practice such as fairness, clarity, chronology, and completeness, this film still provides a world of significant data and arguments—about common women in the market, heroes, traditional roles, social practices, suffering, marriage, and ongoing gaps between rhetoric and reality—that we can recognize as historical. One could even say that, in its own way, it undertakes four of the traditional tasks of history—recounting, explaining, and interpreting the past, and attempting to justify the way it has undertaken those tasks.

The film recounts the lives of (some) Vietnamese women over the last twenty years, showing the effects of revolution at home and emigration to America. It explains that underneath surface changes—e.g., women can now become engineers and doctors—continuities from the past such as Confucianism and patriarchy still have a major role in defining women's activities and lives. It interprets the female-male struggle as ageless and ongoing, something that continues to occur no matter what the new social order or national context. And it justifies itself by dejustifying the traditional form of the historical documentary and suggesting that the forms of our knowledge about the past need to be changed. How else to explain the inclusion of data that do no more than add texture to the portrait—memories of the taste of ice cream in Viet Nam, dreamy images of moonlight on rivers, love songs and lullabies?

Ultimately, *Surname Viet Given Name Nam* refuses notions of causation or development and creates history through poetic overlays of sounds, images, words, ideas. Certainly its historical world overflows with recurrent images and themes: Women and dance. Women and marriage. Women as mothers. Women and sacrifice. Women and war. Women and boats. Women as heroes. Women and sex. Women and song. Women and revolution. Women and exile. If in exploring these themes, the film raises many more questions than it can possibly answer, this too may be seen as part of a new approach to the past, a method that provides yet another critique of patriarchal historical practice, in which ambiguity and doubt are always replaced by certitude.[15]

Outtake: The postmodern historical film is not (yet) a genre, nor a movement, nor even (heaven help us) a trend. Perhaps it is best seen as a tendency—a growing tendency. If exemplars are still limited, it is important to emphasize that the five works described above represent neither the sum total of nor the full range of possibilities for this new kind of history. Among other examples of the tendency, let me add:

Women's History: Mitzi Goldman's and Trish FitzSimons's *Snakes and Ladders* (1987). A history of higher education for women in Australia which, taking the child's game of the title as both its central metaphor and narrative strategy, does not insert women into a conventional historical framework, but forsakes linearity in favor of a multivoiced work that is both open-ended and self-questioning.[16]

Labor history: Kevin Duggan's *Paterson* (1988). An often lyrical work that mixes many elements—events in the present and in the past, documentary footage and dramatized fictional scenes, poetic evocation and traditional hard-nosed realism—as it probes the questions of what, whether, and how past union battles and major strikes (in this case the Paterson silk strike of 1913) can mean to working people today.[17]

Political Biography: Raoul Peck's *Lumumba: Death of a*

Prophet (1992) manipulates time and chronology in what seems to be the manner of an African *griot* or oral historian. Its images and narration shift effortlessly from past to present, from the public sphere to the private, from historical data to the filmmaker's personal ruminations in a work that is at once a visual and an oral meditation on the brief life of Patrice Lumumba and on the promise of African independence, thirty years ago and today.[18]

Social Biography: Terese Svoboda's and Steve Bull's *Margaret Sanger: A Public Nuisance* (1992). Underscored by a jaunty ragtime piano, this sound film is shot in the style of the silent era, with contemporary reenactments that are as grainy and scratchy as its archival footage. In its presentation and historical analysis, the work can be unabashedly funny, using a team of pie-in-the-face vaudevillians to comment upon serious events surrounding Sanger's life and the birth of birth control in America.[19]

Intellectual Biography: John Hughes's *One-Way Street* (1992). Composed in accordance with Walter Benjamin's own ideas of history, knowledge, fragmentation, modernism, the priority of images, and the difficulties of narrative, this film about Benjamin's life shuffles and reshuffles images, text fragments, dramatic reenactments, talking heads, and archival footage into a cinematic version of one of the philosopher's own essays.[20]

These should be enough examples to suggest a larger point: that postmodern historical films are made everywhere these days—in the United States, Europe,

Australia, Latin America, and Africa. Most of them are
low-budget works shot for the small screen. Most
grow out of the documentary tradition, though the
inclusion of dramatized episodes has become a common enough practice. Occasionally a feature-length
dramatic work of history will fulfill notions of postmodernism—say, Alex Cox's *Walker* (1987), an absurdist and overtly anachronist account of the invasion of Nicaragua in 1854 by a troop of Americans led
by William Walker, or Carlos Diegues's *Quilombo*
(1984), which gives us history as musical spectacle as
it presents the grim story of Palmares, a country created by runaway slaves in the jungles of Brazil in the
sixteenth century. Occasionally a cinematic work of
postmodern history may achieve a big reputation (but
still have a small audience)—say, Hans Jürgen Syberberg's six-and-a-half-hour work, *Hitler, a Film from Germany* (1977). Occasionally touches we can call postmodern will inflect an otherwise conventional
narrative film—say, Paul Verhoeven's *The Nasty Girl*
(1990). But for the most part, the postmodern historical film is little known to the general (or even the
scholarly) public because the economics of production
and distribution work to keep any offbeat movements,
trends, or tendencies in film buried. My hope is that
by naming and describing them, I can begin to create
a larger audience for these suggestive works which
open up for all of us new possibilities for historical
representation and understanding.

Why Call it History? Because such films are serious
about describing and understanding, in however un-

usual a form, the beliefs, ideas, experiences, events, movements, and moments of the past. Because they accept the notion that the weight of the past has somehow helped to shape (us in) the present, even if they are not certain about how to assess that weight. Because even though they refuse to think in terms of linear cause and effect, or to accept the idea that chronology is necessarily useful, and even though they insist that past material is always personal, partial, political, problematic, it is still possible to see them fulfilling traditional tasks of history and telling histories—of Solidarity as seen from America; of the Japanese internment camps as seen through the experiences of one family; of Australia in terms of its landscape, real and imagined; of Vienna just before the empire collapsed; of Vietnamese women since the revolution.

A Random Conclusion to a Random Sort of History: Postmodern history is history that does not necessarily call itself History. It is history practiced by people who do not necessarily call themselves Historians with a capital *H* or even a little *h.*

Postmodern history is serious about making current meaning from the traces of the past. But it (obviously) suspects logic, linearity, progression, and completeness as ways of rendering that past.

Postmodern history weds theory and practice, the pulse of the past and ways of thinking about how that pulse means. It is always conscious of itself as a search of the past for present meaning.

Postmodern historians desire to free themselves

from the constricting bonds of metanarratives and historical discipline (the way history is taught in schools). They are visually oriented people who attempt to make the past count in their, and our, lives once again. (The mainstream documentary or dramatic film, with its sense of a linear and completed moral story, would be suitable as a visual form for anyone who finds the discipline and its metanarratives satisfactory.)

Postmodern historians have not given up on the past or history—only on History as professionalized and institutionalized, History as a support for a social and intellectual order whose foundations perpetually need to be questioned.

Postmodern history makes us rethink the possibilities for history—indeed, these films are a beginning of such rethinking—and for creating a new kind of relationship to the past. That we may not fully understand their contribution (an important word for historians) can be explained by what Jean-François Lyotard says in another context about creative artists: one may see the work of postmodern historians as in part a search for the rules by which their sense and practice of history will eventually be judged.[21]

Addendum: The recent debate surrounding the possibility of representing the history of the Holocaust impinges upon the notion of the postmodern historical film. Whether it is the historian Saul Friedländer lamenting the possibility of finding a rational explanation for events so monumentally irrational, or Jean-François Lyotard demanding that historians of

Auschwitz lend an ear *to what is not presentable under the rules of knowledge,* or Hayden White claiming that only modernism in historical writing can handle the modernism of Auschwitz—the result is a sense that traditional history in this century has run up against the limits of representation.[22]

One way around these limits has been suggested by White, who calls for a telling of the past in a new voice that lies somewhere between the objective voice of scholarship and the subjective voice of fiction and poetry. This *intransitive middle voice* would be that of the historian, not describing and analyzing but encountering and experiencing events of the past. Such a voice is, if one adds a visual component, precisely that of the filmmakers whose works are described here as postmodern history, a voice that continually interrogates the facts, fictions, and memories of the past, and also interrogates itself. It is a voice that is part of a continuing desire of people who wish to understand the past. A voice that refuses to take as the lesson of Auschwitz the notion that an understanding of the past is no longer possible. A voice that ignores the question of whether or not history is a rational discourse describing rational phenomena. A voice that knows that as part of our humanity we can never stop the effort to talk about and make meaning of the past.

· 10 ·

What You Think About

When You Think about Writing a Book on History and Film

Exposure to the medium of film, especially in its innovative forms, can have a subversive effect upon the historian. So many techniques of film (like those of modernist and postmodernist writing) seem to cry out for use by the scholar. Montage, intercutting, collage, the mixing of genres, the creative interaction of fact and fiction, history, memory, and autobiography—why are these not part of the (re)presentational modes of the historian as narrator or essayist?

Make it personal. The story of a quest. Desire to understand if and how (but mostly how) the film medium can be (and has been) used to talk about the past.

Admit all the problems involved. That this should not be a written document but a visual one. That one should write about film in film. That words are an especially difficult (impossible?) way of talking about film, without boring people to tears with details of plot and analyses of film language. That it will be necessary to find/create a way of talking about film in words that will not bore me and will somehow communicate the meaning and feeling of the historical world of a film the readers have (probably) not seen.

That despite all these problems involved, it remains important to come to grips with the possibilities of the visual media for history.

▼ ▼ ▼

Why the traditional historical film cannot be satisfying as history. Why such works are always compromised. How the conventions of narrative film demand the inclusion of invented dramatic elements that all historians judge fictional. How the problem stems from the model for such films—the written narrative. Which means: the standards of judgment are also taken from written history. Which means: they are inappropriate to the visual medium.

Experimental or postmodernist historical film can create space for a new sort of historical world to grow.

▼ ▼ ▼

We must allow film to collapse historical time (as in Ousmane Sembene's *Ceddo*). Don't we do the same in written history? Skip over centuries of development, warfare, religious or social change in a single sentence or paragraph that summarizes so much material that it becomes virtually meaningless. My favorite example (from a biography of Rosa Luxemburg): "In the four-teenth century Lithuania emerged from obscurity."

▼ ▼ ▼

African historical films provide a good corrective to our own tradition. Take the notion that the *griot* and filmmaker play similar roles, that both carry on the values, standards, customs, myths, and histories of a people or tribe. The *griot* does not of course do history in our sense of the word, but adjusts the story to the audience. Alters the tale in response to responses. Celebrates the past. Glorifies the rulers. Enforces traditional values.

Don't we historians do the same? Can you play jester to the ruling class if there is no ruling class? But there is a ruling ideology. We call it history and how we define it makes all the difference.

Can we allow African filmmakers to play that traditional historical role of *griot?* What does it mean to ask "Can we allow them?" when they are already doing it? Is not all history essentially an appropriation of the experience of others—even ourselves—into categories of understanding that are usually not recognized, and would not be accepted, by the subjects of our study?

The question comes down to how much one wishes to uphold the discourse which we in the West call history. To shift into film—and to accept other filmic traditions—is to look for ways around such appropriative discourse. It is to attempt to allow other traditions space in which to breathe. There are dangers here, yes, but opportunities as well. Surely African filmmakers must be allowed that role of *griot*. Better yet: show that we Western historians are *griots* too!

▼ ▼ ▼

The historical film has not been of much concern to Third World filmmakers. When they have made such films the aim has often been to discover or create a tradition which had not really existed. History as a present and future project. Not just a Third World idea, but ours as well. Black history, women's history, gay history. You name it. Can we expect history to be the same thing in societies which have been historicized by others? Which have suffered from the history of others; from being taught, as were the Africans, that their ancestors were the Gauls (Safi Faye of Senegal shows this in *Fad'jal*, which opens with black schoolchildren repeating phrases about the greatness of their Sun King, Louis XIV).

Question: Would an ethnographic film in a preliterate culture be a historical film for those in that culture?

Question: Do a people have a History if they do not have the concept of "history" in their tradition?

Question: Will cultures that do not have History have it one day? Is modernity like the Fail, the time when people enter time?

▼ ▼ ▼

What is a historical question? (Necessary to know if we want to know what is an historical answer.) What do we want to know about the past? What can film tell us that we didn't know before? Parallel (in a small way) to Foucault and historians: What was he asking us to think about that we had not thought about before?

Questions posed by historical films:

1. *Frida* (Paul Leduc—Mexico): What is a life? How does it mean?
2. *Walker* (Alex Cox—U.S.): What is it to talk about the past and present at the same time?
3. *Sans Soleil* (Chris Marker—U.S.-France): What is it to consider a century in which the visual media take the place of memory?
4. *Surname Viet Given Name Nam* (Trinh T. Minh-ha—U.S.): What is it to talk about women's identity? In a culture? Across cultures?
5. *Quilombo* (Carlos Diegues—Brazil): What is it to represent the spirit rather than the literal look of the past?
6. *Ceddo* (Ousmane Sembene—Senegal): How can we bypass the norms of written history and transfer oral history directly to the screen?
7. *Die Patriotin* (Alexander Kluge—Germany): What does it mean to search for history? What does it mean to want history to mean?
8. *Far from Poland* (Jill Godmilow—U.S.): What does it mean to understand events in a land that we cannot visit? (Which also includes the past.)

None of this is history in the traditional sense, but rather history in a new visual sense. History that moots the issue of whether it competes with written history. History that stands—perhaps—adjacent to written history. Another way of thinking about the past.

The real subject of the book is not the historical film, but the new sorts of history that are made possible by the medium of film. The new ways of thinking about the past.

▼ ▼ ▼

Our interest in history and in narrative history depends in part upon its art, in part upon its research, and in part upon its conceptualization. (Not that the three can be separated.) What is missing in the standard historical (illusionist realist) film is the density of research and conceptualization. But in a good historical film, these are present, though one must allow for different kinds of research and different kinds of conceptualization.

One cannot understand the levels of complexity that a film reaches unless one has some understanding of the language in which it speaks.

▼ ▼ ▼

Old Gringo is the kind of Hollywood historical film that one thinks must be dead and buried, so quaint (and racist) is it in language and contents. With poor Mexican peasants and whores speaking perfect, if slightly accented, English, and Yanquis being trashed for not understanding the passion of Latins, and the white woman finding her dark lover, and passionate *bailes* day and night—they have so much more fun than we do, these dark and not completely clean folks who are fighting for a heroic cause which we know is noble but which they can never ultimately win, or we wouldn't be able to go on making films like this. The position of the historian vis-à-vis the traditional historical film is the same as that of Third World and avant-garde filmmakers. Together we must learn about possibilities of a different, more interesting visual past; together we must learn how to think visually about historical questions.

Is the movement of a tree in the wind history? The shape of a hat? Or of a hut? The gesture of a man when he rises? These too are questions to ask. Cannot such pieces of data also be used in written history, used because they have some meaning beyond their mere brute reality? And are they not essential in a historical film? And how are we to understand what they mean?

▼ ▼ ▼

There is a perpetual struggle in film between those who want to make it a serious way of communicating (truth, cultural values either high or low, traditions, history) and those who see it only as packaged entertainment (with, no doubt, positions staked out along a line between the two). Another way of phrasing it: Hollywood (with its suburbs in Rome, Manila, Bombay, etc.) versus the rest of the world. My work locates itself within that struggle, within what has to be the losing—or at the very least—the minority side. One might add: a perpetual minority. For clearly film will never be used primarily as a serious medium of either high or popular or folk culture. So what?

Or is it really true that postmodernism collapses such distinctions? The critical language about postmodernism would have you believe this, but what sort of language is it? A rarified language that not only shuts out the public at large but most of the scholarly community as well. A language that can only be understood by a specialized elite. Thus the discourse of postmodernism is always outside the terrain it describes. As is my own (simpler, less jargon-ridden, but equally theoretical) writing on history and film. The problem: how to speak of that terrain from within. The (possible) answer: use film.

▼ ▼ ▼

Groucho put it this way: I wouldn't want to belong to any club that would admit me as a member.

▼ ▼ ▼

It's bad enough to write about film—but to write in the first person . . .

["To begin with, naturally, would be about myself"— the first line of my grandfather's memoir.]

▼ ▼ ▼

The book must be in many voices. About the problems it tackles. About history. About film. About itself. Its own raison d'être.

Is it that we expect the film to be a window onto the past? To show us exactly how things were? A book, too?

But the book hides itself and the fact that a historian made it. So does the illusionist-realist film.

History is a story that makes an argument. That *is* an argument. Written history does not just show the past. It shows parts of the past determined by later knowledge of why that past, those details, are important.

By definition, it knows more than the participants could ever have known at the time—

[The same is true for my grandfather's view of his life. We do not read his story as it was lived, but as fragments he could remember in the Jewish Hospital of Hope seventy years after the events. There is no story of his life apart from those intervening years. No story that does not include that hospital ward and his strokes and heart attacks and the person who transcribed his words . . .

To begin with, naturally, would be about myself. And about all those others too.]

▾ ▾ ▾

The character of William Walker exists on the screen because the director Alex Cox (a shorthand way of referring to a lot of people involved in this project) wants him to exist.

Question: How do the overt anachronisms in *Walker* violate our sense of history? Answer: they don't. The anachronisms merely acknowledge that the past can exist only in light of the present.

Indeed, one must argue the other way. Walker's invasion of Nicaragua in the 1850s must be set in the context of Viet Nam, Zippo lighters, Mercedes-Benz automobiles, helicopters, Sandinistas, and Contras. To do otherwise is to cripple ourselves in our knowledge of the past. To mystify the present. To claim that history can somehow exist in a vacuum that excludes our knowledge of history's future.

▼ ▼ ▼

The challenge is this: the visual media—or some people who have used film—propose new ways of thinking about our past. These ways are unsettling because they escape the confines of words and provide elements—visual, aural, emotional, subconscious—that we don't know how to admit into our knowledge. There is something about the moving image and the way it means that seems to escape the confines of words (including these). To mean more and to mean differently than the words can say. This is not just to admit a major problem of my own work—that any written description of a film seems less than a pale ghost of the experience of the film. It is also to assert that all critical apparatus of film theory/criticism/

history is also no more than the palest reflection of the experience and meaning of a film, and thus curiously beside the point.

Is this writing, then, not a pale ghost, not beside the point? Perhaps. But in a way it does not have a point. Its point is not to have a point but to point. Its point is not to capture that elusive image but to point at it and beyond it. To get you to look at the possible histories that unfold upon the screen. To point to a series of new pasts. To suggest that film forces us to live in a most uncomfortable sort of world—a world in which we cannot control or contain our past with words; cannot tame its full meanings within the discipline of a discourse because the meanings themselves—encoded as images as well as words—ultimately elude words. (The unruly meanings of the past trouble written history as well, but here we feel we can tame them because words at least seem adequate to the control of words.) With film the cat of our meaning cannot be placed back into the bag of discipline. If we are honest we can never again deny the arbitrary nature of that discipline. And thus of the meanings we insist it must carry.

[To begin with, naturally, would be about myself.]

History on film, then, seems to be about loss of control; loss of sense; loss . . . But the pointing will also be to its gains. The new ways it can raise issues, debate them. The incorporation of mystery, beauty, human gesture into our notion of the past. For the past did not just mean—it sounded and looked and moved as well. A sunset may not be part of history, but sunsets have had meaning for people; have soothed hearts, raised hopes, calmed fears. Surely this is part of history.

[To begin with, naturally, would be about myself.]

▼ ▼ ▼

We live within the discourse of historical answers for which we desperately need new questions.

▼ ▼ ▼

These Paradoxes:

1. Popular historical films, that is, those which might carry historical consciousness of a postliterate culture, are historically shallow and visually uninteresting. Suffer from same problem as certain sorts of "old-fashioned" history. Suffer from both intellectual and aesthetic anemia.
2. Avant-garde historical films will not interest many people: hence cannot possibly solve crises of cultural communication; cannot be a tool for holding postliterate culture together.
3. To someone (me) interested in the possibilities of history on film, it is impossible not to desire the most interesting kinds of film, the most intellectually and artistically complex works.
4. Solution to this problem: none.

▼ ▼ ▼

Historians are people who spend their lives answering questions that nobody has asked.

▼ ▼ ▼

We must recognize that film will create different sorts of projects, pose different sorts of questions and give different sorts of answers from written history. Which means: film will carry different sorts of data. Will undertake different sorts of analysis. Will, ultimately, create a different sort of historical world.

The work of understanding film language and the structure of a historical film world must be part of the problem and interest of history on film. Which means: the data cannot be unhinged from the way they are presented if one is to come to grips fully with the visual historical realm.

Take this lesson back to written history.

▼ ▼ ▼

The best historical films will:

1. Show not just what happened in the past but how what happened means to us.
2. Interrogate the past for the sake of the present. Remember that historians are working for the living, not for the dead.
3. Create a historical world complex enough so that it overflows with meaning; so that its meanings are always multiple; so that its meanings cannot be contained or easily expressed in words.

What historical film can do:

1. Comment on a tradition of representing the past: *Walker.*

2. Create a spectacle that will carry a particular feeling of how the past means: *Quilombo.*

3. Collapse an oral history tradition into a coherent story which carries out themes spanning large periods of time: *Ceddo.*

4. Ruminate on the possible meanings of historical events or eras, such as disparities of cultures and sense of time in the modern world: *Sans Soleil.*

5. Rethink and re-present the dimensions and ambiguities of a tradition, showing its continuities and ruptures through revolution and emigration: *Surname Viet Given Name Nam.*

6. Question the nature of historical quest itself: *Die Patriotin.*

7. Analyze and question the images of the historical realities we think we know most clearly: *Hitler, a Film from Germany.*

▼ ▼ ▼

Photos and newsreels limit our attempt to feel or see our way into the past, because a sense of nostalgia and change adheres to all such photographic images. This nostalgia immediately signals that we cannot experience what people at the time felt. Most bluntly: they did not know their clothing and automobiles were funny looking; they were instead à la mode. They could not feel the absence of skyscrapers or automobiles. Nor did they live in a gray-and-white or brown-and-white world. The result: new footage, in living color, is more accurate in rendering the past. It carries the notion that the past was in color too, and that our past—since we know our present to be in living color—was not always past but actually had a present too.

▾ ▾ ▾

Films emotionalize the past. Even documentaries too often go overboard with emotion for the exploited and the oppressed. Yet it is not true to say that film can create only emotional but not intellectual truths, while written history does the reverse. Written narrative is hardly devoid of emotion. Repressed emotion colors the value judgments and points of view that suffuse all narrative. The choice and creation of the problems to be studied. The framing of the story. The language used—especially by those who can use it well and who wish to use it with passion. Nor is it necessary that film play so deeply on the emotions. Counterexamples abound in African, European, and Latin American cinema, where a distancing of emotion occurs through film and acting technique; where the emotional tug we associate with American film is missing.

That tug is melodrama. The substitution of certain overwrought forms of emotion for a deeper understanding of personal and social realities. A way of blinding ourselves to social, political, economic—even personal—analysis and understanding. Yet melodrama has been the dominant mode of the Hollywood historical film, thus a major source of criticisms of the historical film. Just the facts, ma'am. The feelings make me blush.

▼ ▼ ▼

What historical film can do: *Walker.*

1. Comment on a tradition of representation and interpretation. Show how it comments on a world of other historical texts.
2. Suggest larger historical moment/movement through a biographical study that reaches beyond a life.
3. Raise this issue: How much information is necessary to make a historical argument? What sort of data? Must it be literal? Can it be symbolic and metaphoric? Part of a larger issue: To what extent is all historical data at once symbolic and metaphorical?

▼ ▼ ▼

Historical films are more than vehicles for delivering data or making an argument. They are new ways of visioning the past. New ways of meeting the material of the past, of interrogating the past for the present. Their meaning can hardly be fixed and simple.

Film has been used too much simply to tell stories from the past. Doing so, it suffers from all the problems of a simply narratized past. Which means reducing options to a single story line.

▼ ▼ ▼

In *Monty Python and the Holy Grail* a modern-day policeman arrests Launcelot for walking around in medieval getup and carrying a sword. That cop has the right idea about history on film.

▼ ▼ ▼

There is no doubt that filmmakers—even the best and most serious—have defined history in a different way from historians. How to put it simply? Filmmakers are less concerned with empirical truth. They are more willing to use the past for some special ends. Or at least more overtly willing to admit they are doing so than any academic historian can or will admit to doing.

Saying this hardly settles the issue. For there are very real differences in the way history has been used in film. Hollywood often uses the past as a setting for romance, to reinforce the status quo. Third World and other serious filmmakers have overtly used history in favor of social change. The question: Which do we prefer?

Even if they have tinkered with or ignored data in a way that no written historian could accept, filmmakers might (or could) have used such data to make the same arguments. Some films—*Ceddo* and *Quilombo* are good examples—represent or parallel real schools or traditions of historical interpretation.

Even when these films do not get the data exactly right, they show a way of looking at history that transcends their shortcomings. Thus they are models of possible histories on film. Models that historians interested in the past (as opposed to the profession) and filmmakers interested in history (rather than profits) might/must/may consider in future undertakings.

▾ ▾ ▾

Sans Soleil opens with an image of three children on a rural road in Iceland, an image the narrator says represents, for the filmmaker, "happiness." It is an image he has been waiting for years to place in a film. An image that is both the theme (and dream) of this century and of all films. This century's dream is immediately undercut by the next shot: the screen goes black, then shows a military airplane rising to the deck of the aircraft carrier. This century's nightmare.

▾ ▾ ▾

A knowledge of the process of creation of a historical work is necessarily part of the meaning delivered by the work. You cannot understand the work in its full dimensions if you do not understand the assumptions and forms of its production. Certainly this becomes most obvious with history on film. Reading through the work thus adds a vital dimension to a reading of the work. (This means, of course, that the meaning is not just in the data delivered but the form of the vehicle of delivery, and its form of production, which mirrors the assumptions and values of the social order producing such a work.)

How worn out seems the old historical vocabulary; how impossibly dense the newer language of film criticism. What does it really mean for a historian to speak of "broader social issues" (the old language)? And yet the current critical language has its own problems with breadth. For it does not simply mean, it seems to overmean, to drown the possibility of meaning in a kind of hyper-rhetoric. As if the apparatus for each sentence overwhelms the meaning which can be possibly communicated by the words used. In short: the elephant gives birth to the mouse.

▾ ▾ ▾

Critics who scorn the possibility of history on film have refused to take the avant-garde film seriously. They are part of that unspoken conspiracy of critics and the film industry which will not look beyond the Hollywood film for meaning. The parallel with written history would be to take popular historians for serious ones. These critics fall into the trap of accepting a commodified medium as the way the medium must be rather than looking beyond to its exploratory possibilities. Which means they refuse to accept the possibility of change in either history or in film. (No doubt the filmmakers of Eastern Europe would disagree with them.)

▾ ▾ ▾

A serious history on film has only recently become possible for lots of reasons: The demise of the studio system in Hollywood. Hollywood today. The challenge to Western political and cultural hegemony. The breakup of empire. The Third World. Minorities within empire. Women. The needs of some countries for self-definition. Government funding. Independent cinema. Lighter, cheaper equipment. New (postmodern) aesthetics. The New History.

We have changed the nature of history radically, but not the nature of the consciousness and the form which expresses that history. What really happens when, say, women's view of the past is expressed in narrative or cinematic forms created by Western white males? The opportunity now is for a new way of seeing the past. More radical because it breaks with form and not just content. And while this could be done in print, it seems easier with the resources of the new medium. Besides, this new filmic history has already been expressed in Germany, Latin America, Africa—even in the United States. Our job is to find out how it is expressed and what this expression means, so that we can learn to criticize. To think. To do. To see.

▼ ▼ ▼

The traditional film, like the traditional narrative history, hides its own constructed nature. Modernist and postmodernist film highlights its constructed nature. This forces (or is meant to force) the spectator to consider the problematics of the form and thus the problematics of the meaning. The result when applied to the historical film: a deeper, more complex intellectual endeavor. Such as the works of Kluge, Syberberg, Cox, Marker, Diegues, et al. Film is so obviously constructed of bits and pieces that to view any film is to face the issue of the production of meaning. One might say that it is written history's ability to escape this question that makes so much history uninteresting to read—a collection of details that are of interest only if one is already interested in those details.

The point: we must come to grips with the production of historical meaning at the same time that we come to grips with the data that produce the meaning.

▼ ▼ ▼

Begin in the first person. Not comfortable writing theory, and yet film studies is dominated by theory. My need to bring this theory down to earth, to personalize, humanize, historicize it. To admit that as a historian, I believe in the reality of the signified—which is to say, the world. Believe that empirical facts exist and insist that if we let go of that belief then we are no longer historians. But also believe that there are an infinite number of ways to deal with our data and what it means. And that in doing so, the literal and the symbolic overlap. This is true in written history but absolutely inescapable with regard to the historical film, where the constructed nature of screen reality can never be forgotten.

Notes

Sources

Acknowledgments

Index

Notes

▼ ▼ ▼

Introduction

1. Peter Novick, *That Noble Dream: The "Objectivity Question" and the American Historical Profession* (New York: Cambridge University Press, 1988), 194.

2. The book was published as *Mirror in the Shrine: American Encounters with Meiji Japan* (Cambridge, Mass.; Harvard University Press, 1988).

3. Published in English as *Cinema and History* (Detroit: Wayne State University Press, 1988).

4. *The Film in History: Restaging the Past* (Totowa, N.J.: Barnes & Noble Imports, 1980).

1. History in Images / History in Words

1. A few historians such as Daniel Walkowitz, Robert Brent Toplin, and R. J. Raack have become deeply involved in filmmaking projects. For an interesting insight into some of the problems of the historian as filmmaker, see Daniel Walkowitz, "Visual History: The Craft of the Historian-Filmmaker," *The Public Historian* 7 (1985): 53–64.

2. Siegfried Kracauer, *Theory of Film: The Redemption of Physical Reality* (New York: Oxford University Press, 1960), 77–79.

3. By now any list of articles, books, and panels on film would be very long. Perhaps the most important symposia were the ones at New York University on October 30, 1982, and the one sponsored by the AHA in Washington, D.C., on April 30–May 1, 1985. The former resulted in Barbara Abrash and Janet Sternberg, eds., *Historians and Filmmakers: Toward Collaboration* (New York: Institute for Research in History 1983), and the latter in John O'Connor, ed., *Image as Artifact: The Historical Analysis of Film and Television* (Malabar, Fla.: R. E. Krieger, 1990). By far the largest meeting on the topic was entitled "Telling the Story: The Media, the Public, and American History," which took place in Boston on April 23–24, 1993. Sponsored by the New England Foundation for the Humanities, this public conference was attended by more than eight hundred people, a large percentage of whom were academic historians or film and video professionals. The proceedings have been published under the same title (Boston: New England Foundation for the Humanities, 1995).

4. R. J. Raack, "Historiography as Cinematography: A Prolegomenon to Film Work for Historians," *Journal of Contemporary History* 18 (1983): 416, 418.

5. I. C. Jarvie, "Seeing through Movies," *Philosophy of the Social Sciences 8 (1978): 378.*

6. Raack, "Historiography as Cinematography," 416.

7. Jarvie, "Seeing through Movies," 378.

8. Seymour Chatman, "What Novels Can Do That Films Can't (and Vice Versa)," *Critical Inquiry* 7 (1980): 125–126.

9. Pierre Sorlin argues the value of film in giving a feeling for certain kinds of setting in "Historical Films as Tools for Historians," in O'Connor, ed., *Image as Artifact.*

10. Hayden White has made this point in a number of works, including *Metahistory: The Historical Imagination in Nineteenth-Century Europe* (Baltimore: Johns Hopkins University

Press, 1973), and in various articles in *Tropics of Discourse: Essays in Cultural Criticism* (Baltimore: Johns Hopkins University Press, 1978).

11. A good survey of recent film theory is Dudley Andrew, *Concepts in Film Theory* (New York: Oxford University Press, 1984).

12. Quotations from the narration of *Sans Soleil.*

13. See Teshome H. Gabriel, *Third Cinema in the Third World: The Aesthetics of Liberation,* (Ann Arbor: VMI Research Press, 1982), and Roy Armes, *Third World Film Making and the West* (Berkeley: University of California Press, 1987), esp. 87–100.

14. For a full discussion of *Ceddo* see Gabriel, *Third Cinema in the Third World,* 86–89, and Armes, *Third World Film Making:* 290–291. For *Quilombo,* see Coco Fusco, "Choosing Between Legend and History: An Interview with Carlos Diegues," and Robert Stam, *"Quilombo,"* both in *Cineaste* 15 (1986): 12–14, 42–44.

15. "The Burden of History," *History and Theory* 5 (1966): 110–134, esp. 126–127, 131. This article is also reprinted in *Tropics of Discourse,* 27–50.

16. Hayden White has made this argument in a number of articles. See, for example, "Historical Text as Literary Artifact" and "Historicism, History, and Figurative Imagination," both in *Tropics of Discourse,* 81–120.

17. Bill Nichols, *Ideology and the Image* (Bloomington: Indiana University Press, 1981), 243.

2. The Historical Film

1. Quoted in Peter Novick, *That Noble Dream,* 194.

2. There is no single book that satisfactorily covers the topic of history and film. The broadest discussion takes place in a forum in *American Historical Review* 93 (1988): 1173–1227, which includes the following articles: Robert A. Rosenstone, "History in Images/History in Words: Reflections on the Possibility of Really Putting History onto Film" (Chapter 1 of this

volume); David Herlihy, "Am I a Camera? Other Reflections on Film and History"; Hayden White, "Historiography and Historiophoty"; John J. O'Connor, "History in Images/Images in History: Reflections on the Importance of Film and Television Study for an Understanding of the Past"; Robert Brent Toplin, "The Filmmaker as Historian."

3. White, "Historiography and Historiophoty," 1193.

4. John E. O'Connor and Martin A. Jackson, eds., *American History/American Film: Interpreting the Hollywood Image* (New York: Ungar, 1979).

5. Natalie Zemon Davis, "'Any Resemblance to Persons Living or Dead': Film and the Challenge of Authenticity," *Yale Review* 76 (1987): 457–482.

6. Natalie Zemon Davis, *The Return of Martin Guerre* (Cambridge, Mass.: Harvard University Press, 1983), viii.

7. Daniel J. Walkowitz, "Visual History: The Craft of the Historian-Filmmaker," *Public Historian* 7 (Winter 1985): 57.

8. Books on the Mississippi Freedom Summer include Doug McAdam, *Freedom Summer* (New York: Oxford University Press, 1988), and Mary A. Rothschild, *A Case of Black and White: Northern Volunteers and the Southern Freedom Summers, 1964–1965* (Westport, Conn.: Greenwood Press, 1982). For an older account that remains useful, see Len Holt, *The Summer That Didn't End* (New York: Morrow, 1965).

9. For a history of the Fifty-fourth Regiment, see Peter Burchard, *One Gallant Rush: Robert Gould Shaw and His Brave Black Regiment* (New York: St. Martin's Press, 1965).

10. James McPherson, "The *Glory* Story," *New Republic* 202 (January 8, 1990): 22–27.

3. *Reds* as History

This essay has benefited from conversations with my friends and fellow historians Joseph Boskin, David J. Fisher, and Clayton Koppes, and I wish to thank them for sharing their ideas with me.

1. Robert Rosenstone, *Romantic Revolutionary* (Cambridge, Mass.: Harvard University Press, 1990).

6. Walker

1. In the United States, *Walker* is distributed in 35 mm by Universal, and has been released on video by MCA Home Video.

2. The basic works from the period are William Walker, *The War in Nicaragua* (New York: Goetzel, 1860; facsimile edition, Tucson: University of Arizona Press, 1985), and William V. Wells, *Walker's Expedition to Nicaragua* (New York: Stringer and Townsend, 1856). Book-length accounts of Walker in English include James J. Roche, *The Story of the Filibusters* (London: Unwin, 1891); William O. Scroggs, *Filibusters and Financiers* (New York: Macmillan, 1916); Lawrence Greene, *The Filibuster: The Career of William Walker* (Indianapolis: Bobbs-Merrill, 1937); Albert Z. Carr, *The World and William Walker* (New York: Harper and Row, 1963); Noel B. Gerson, *Sad Swashbuckler: The Life of William Walker* (New York: Thomas Nelson, 1976); Frederick Rosengarten, *Freebooters Must Die* (Wayne, Penn.: Haverford Press, 1976). Books with chapters on Walker include E. Alexander Powell, "The King of the Filibusters," in *Gentlemen Rovers* (New York: Scribner's, 1913); Abdullah Achmed, "William Walker," in *Dreamers of Empire* (New York: Stokes, 1929); David I. Folkman, *The Nicaragua Route* (Salt Lake City: University of Utah Press, 1972); Robert E. May, *The Southern Dream of a Caribbean Empire, 1854–1861* (Baton Rouge: Louisiana State University Press, 1973). Spanish-language sources on Walker are rich, and include Lorenzo Montufar y Rivera Maestre, *Walker en Centro America*, 2 vols. (Guatemala: Tipografia 'La Union', 1887); Alejandro Hurtado Chamorro, *William Walker: Ideales y propositos* (Granada: Centro America, 1965); Enrique Guier, *William Walker* (San José, Costa Rica: Tipografia Lehmann, 1971).

3. Powell, *Gentlemen Rovers*, ix.

4. Scroggs, *Filibusters and Financiers*, 396.
5. Greene, *The Filibuster*, 117.

7. Sans Soleil

1. Seven years after completing the essay, the exact sources for some of the quotations in this paragraph elude me. Most of them can be found in Steven Simmons, "Man without a Country," *The Movies* (November 1983) and Terrence Rafferty, "Marker Changes Trains," both of which are quoted in the April 3, 1987 issue of *History through Film and Video*, an occasional publication of the International House of Philadelphia.

2. Janine Marchessault, *"Sans Soleil," CineAction* 5 (May 1986), 3.

3. All quotations taken from an unpublished typescript of the soundtrack of *Sans Soleil*.

8. Re-visioning History

1. Roy Armes, *Third World Film Making*, 99.
2. This essay will bypass the issue of who exactly is "author" of a motion picture. For practical purposes, I shall name directors as the individuals responsible for given works. Given the point of this essay, to investigate the many ways of doing historical films, the concept of who is responsible for a film is not really important anyway. It should, however, be pointed out that many of the authors of the books mentioned here discuss the problem. Even those who do not believe that the director is really the "auteur" of a motion picture find themselves utilizing the concept. It's a difficult one to avoid. Perhaps the best explanation comes from Timothy Corrigan in *New German Film: The Displaced Image* (Austin: University of Texas Press, 1983): "While this investigation uses this notion as a hermeneutical device and the filmmakers often exploit it as a distribution strategy, it is certainly not . . . an entirely suitable

classifier but rather an often grudgingly accepted image that aids communication."

3. Françoise Pfaff, *Twenty-Five Black African Filmmakers* (Westport, Conn.: Greenwood, 1988), ix–x.

4. Quoted in Françoise Pfaff, *The Cinema of Ousmane Sembene* (Westport, Conn.: Greenwood, 1984), 29.

5. Ibid., 166.

6. Julianne Burton, ed., *Cinema and Social Change in Latin America: Conversations with Filmmakers* (Austin: University of Texas Press, 1986), xi.

7. Ibid., xii.

8. Ibid.

9. Michael Chahan, *The Cuban Image: Cinema and Cultural Politics in Cuba* (Bloomington: Indiana University Press, 1985), 248.

10. Quoted in Randal Johnson and Robert Stam, *Brazilian Cinema* (Austin: University of Texas Press, 1988), 50.

11. Ibid., 224.

12. Quoted in Corrigan, *New German Film*, 7.

13. Ibid., 147.

14. Anton Kaes, *From Hitler to Heimat: The Return of History as Film* (Cambridge, Mass.: Harvard University Press, 1989), xi.

15. Kaes, *Hitler to Heimat*, 49.

16. Ibid.

17. Ibid., 111.

9. Film and the Beginnings of Postmodern History

1. Similar "amateur" experiments in seeing the past anew and creating a sort of postmodern history also seem to be taking place in other fields, such as theater, performance art, and dance. But on an international level it is easier to track and experience such changes in the visual media, which circulate so easily around the world.

2. Pauline Marie Rosenau, *Post-Modernism and the Social Sciences* (Princeton: Princeton University Press, 1992), 63.

3. Quotations taken, in order, from the following: Linda Hutcheon, *A Poetic of Postmodernism: History, Theory, Fiction* (New York: Routledge, 1988), 89, 74; Elizabeth Deeds Emarth, *Sequel to History: Postmodernism and the Crisis of Representational Time* (Princeton: Princeton University Press, 1992), 12, 41, 14, 8; F. R. Ankersmit, "Historiography and Postmodernism," *History and Theory* 28, no. 2 (1989): 149–151. See also Hans Kellner, "Beautifying the Nightmare: The Aesthetics of Postmodern History," *Strategies* 4/5 (1991): 289–313.

4. Hutcheon, *A Poetic of Postmodernism*, 91–95.

5. Rosenau, *Post-Modernism and the Social Sciences*, 66.

6. Gertrude Himmelfarb, "Telling it as you like it: Postmodernist history and the flight from fact," *Times Literary Supplement* (October 16, 1992).

7. Presumably, Himmelfarb is attacking Scott for her work, *Gender and the Politics of History* (New York: Columbia University Press, 1988) and Zeldin for his two-volume study, *France 1848–1945* (London: Oxford University Press, 1972, 1977). The former, a strongly feminist reading of history, is straightforward and traditional in its rhetorical style; the latter is, formally, more unusual—a topically-arranged portrait of France which to some extent moots chronology in favor of a kind of ahistorical "impressionism," Zeldin's effort may be seen as a move towards a new kind of written history that one might wish to label "premature postmodernism."

8. Simon Schama, *Dead Certainties (Unwarranted Speculations)* (New York: Knopf, 1991), 320, 322.

9. There have been a number of attempts at formal innovation in the writing of history in recent years, but these seem largely to have escaped the theorists who have written about postmodern history. For a brief introduction to this tendency, see Robert A. Rosenstone, "Experiments in Writing the Past," *Perspectives* 30 (1992): 10, 12ff.

10. Authored by Roy Rosenszweig, Steve Brier, et al., the work of history, entitled *We Who Built America* (Santa Monica:

Voyager, 1993), is a CD-ROM version of a textbook by the same authors with the same title. Marsha Kinder, *Blood Cinema* (Berkeley: University of California Press, 1993) is a study of recent Spanish cinema that has an accompanying CD-ROM.

11. *Far from Poland* (1984). Directed by Jill Godmilow. Color. 109 minutes. Distributor: Women Make Movies, 462 Broadway, Suite 501, New York, NY 10013.

12. *History and Memory* (1991). Directed by Rea Tajiri. Color/BW. 32 minutes. Distributor: Women Make Movies.

13. *Camera Natura* (1986). Directed by Ross Gibson. Color. 32 minutes. Distributor: Australian Film Commission, Sydney, Australia. A copy of this film, for study but not for circulation, is in the UCLA Film Archive.

14. *Hard Times and Culture—Part 1: "Vienna, Fin de siècle"* (1990). Directed by Juan Downey. Color. 34 minutes. Distributor: Electronic Arts Intermix, Inc., 536 Broadway, New York, NY 10012.

15. *Surname Viet Given Name Nam* (1989). Directed by Trinh T. Minh-ha. Color. 108 minutes. Distributor: Women Make Movies.

16. *Snakes and Ladders* (1987). Directed by Mitzi Goldman and Trish FitzSimons. Color. 59 minutes. Distributor: Women Make Movies.

17. *Paterson* (1988). Directed by Kevin Duggan. Color/BW. 37 minutes. Distributor: Kevin Duggan, Paterson Film Project, 121 Fulton St., 5th Floor, New York, NY 10038.

18. *Lumumba: Death of a Prophet* (1992). Directed by Raoul Peck. Color. 69 minutes. Distributor: California Newsreel, 149 Ninth Street, San Francisco, CA 94103.

19. *Margaret Sanger: A Public Nuisance* (1992). Directed by Terese Svoboda and Steve Bull. Color/BW. 27 minutes. Distributor: Women Make Movies.

20. *One-Way Street* (1992). Directed by John Hughes. Color. 58 minutes. Distributor: Australia Broadcasting Corporation.

21. Jean-François Lyotard, *The Postmodern Condition* (Minneapolis: University of Minnesota Press, 1984), 81.

22. Saul Friedländer and Jean-François Lyotard are both

quoted in Anton Kaes's excellent and suggestive essay, "Holocaust and the End of History: Postmodern Historiography in the Cinema," in Saul Friedländer, ed., *Probing the Limits of Representation: Nazism and the "Final Solution"* (Cambridge, Mass.: Harvard University Press, 1992), 206–222. Hayden White's views may be found in "Historical Emplotment and the Problem of Truth," in the same volume, 37–53.

Sources

▼ ▼ ▼

Chapter 1: "History in Images / History in Words: Reflections on the Possibility of Really Putting History onto Film," *American Historical Review* 93 (Dec. 1988): 1173–1185.

Chapter 2: "Like Writing History with Lightning," *Contention* 2:3 (1993). "The Historical Film: Looking at the Past in a Postliterate Age," in Lloyd Kramer et al., eds., *Learning History in America: Schools, Cultures, and Politics* (Minneapolis: University of Minnesota Press, 1994), 141–160.

Chapter 3: "*Reds* as History," *Reviews in American History* 10 (1982): 299–310.

Chapter 4: "*The Good Fight:* History, Memory, Documentary," *Cineaste* 17: 1 (1989): 12–15.

Chapter 5: "*JFK:* Historical Fact / Historical Film," *American Historical Review* 97 (April 1992): 506–511.

Chapter 6: "*Walker:* The Dramatic Film as (Postmodern) History," in Robert A. Rosenstone, ed., *Revisioning History: Contemporary Filmmakers and the Construction of the Past* (Princeton: Princeton University Press, 1995).

Chapter 8: "Revisioning History: Contemporary Filmmakers and the Construction of the Past," *Comparative Studies in*

Society and History 32 (Oct. 1990): 822–837. Reprinted with the permission of Cambridge University Press.

Chapter 9: "The Future of the Past: Film and the Beginnings of Postmodern History," Vivian Sobchack, ed., *Film and the Problem* (New York: Routledge, 1995).

Chapter 10: "What You Think About When You Think About Writing a Book on History and Film," *Public Culture* 3 (Fall 1990), 49–66. © 1990 by The University of Chicago. All rights reserved.

Acknowledgments

▼ ▼ ▼

The publication of the essays that constitute *Visions of the Past* and of the book itself leaves me in great debt to many institutions and individuals. My heartfelt thanks for invaluable support go to the California Institute of Technology for providing for almost three decades a splendid atmosphere in which to pursue humanistic studies; the Division of Humanities and Social Sciences and its recent chairpersons, David Grether and John Ledyard, for generosity in supporting research and travel; the division administrator Susan Davis, for knowing the devil is in the details and always taking care of them; my colleagues in the humanities, who backed my desire to create a small film program at Caltech; the National Endowment for the Humanities, for a Senior Fellowship and summer stipend that went toward studying film; the Hawaii International Film Festival, its director, Janet Paulsen, and its then adjunct scholars, Frank Tillman and Victor

Kobayashi, who in 1983 forced me to begin thinking about history and film by creating a symposium devoted to that topic; the Neighborhood Television and Film Project of Philadelphia and its superb director, Linda Blackaby, for putting me together with the filmmaker Jill Godmilow and inviting me to express outrageous ideas; the Smithsonian Institution, the New England Foundation for the Humanities, the California Foundation for the Humanities, the California Historical Society, the UCLA Film and Television Archives, the Society for Cinema Studies, the American Studies Association, the American Historical Association, and the Organization of American Historians for providing forums in which to test ideas on history and film; the *American Historical Review* and its editor, David Ransel, for having the vision to open the journal's pages to historical film; filmmakers Noel Buckner, Mary Dore, Sam Sills, Steven Stept, Richard Heus, Ilan Ziv, and Warren Beatty for making me part of their projects; filmmakers Howard Dratch, Jill Godmilow, David Hamilton, Trinh T. Min-ha, Edward James Olmos, Gene Rosow, and Robert M. Young for giving me a deeper sense of how things look from the production side; friends and colleagues for helping with comments and criticism, or for just providing a friendly ear—Barbara Abrash, Nick Dirks, David James Fisher, Doug Flamming, Sumiko Higashi, Min Soo Kang, Clayton Koppes, Morgan Kousser, David Marvit, Maclen Marvit, Bryant Simon, Dan Sipe, Moshe Sluhovsky, Vivian Sobchack, Alice Wexler, and Robert Wohl; my secretary, Sheryl Cobb, for superb work that makes my scholarly life easier, and for handling the important final details in my absence; Aida Donald of Harvard University Press, for once again taking a chance; my editor, Alison Kent, for getting such a quick decision and shepherding the volume through the Press; and Nahid for bringing the most valuable of gifts: hope.

Index

▼ ▼ ▼